Important Instruction

Students, Parents, and Teachers can use the URL or QR code provided below to access two full-length Lumos STAAR practice tests. Please note that these assessments are provided in the Online format only.

URL	QR Code
Visit the URL below and place the book access code **http://www.lumoslearning.com/a/tedbooks** **Access Code: G7MSTAAR-94056-P**	

lumos learning
Developed by Expert Teachers

TEXAS STAAR Test Prep: 7th Grade Math Practice Workbook and Full-length Online Assessments: STAAR Study Guide

Contributing Author   - Aaron Spencer
Contributing Author   - Nikki McGee
Executive Producer   - Mukunda Krishnaswamy
Designer and Illustrator - Vaishnavi K R

ISBN-13: 978-1-949855-33-3

Printed in the United States of America

For permissions and additional information contact us

Lumos Information Services, LLC
PO Box 1575, Piscataway, NJ 08855-1575
http://www.LumosLearning.com

Email: support@lumoslearning.com
Tel: (732) 384-0146
Fax: (866) 283-6471

Developed by Expert Teachers

INTRODUCTION

This book is specifically designed to improve student achievement on the State of Texas Assessment of Academic Readiness (STAAR). With over a decade of expertise in developing practice resources for standardized tests, Lumos Learning has designed the most efficient methodology to help students succeed on the state assessments (See Figure 1).

Lumos Smart Test Prep provides students STAAR assessment rehearsal along with an efficient pathway to overcome any standards proficiency gaps. Students perform at their best on standardized tests when they feel comfortable with the test content as well as the test format. Lumos online practice tests are meticulously designed to mirror the STAAR assessment. It adheres to the guidelines provided by the STAAR for the number of questions, standards, difficulty level, sessions, question types, and duration.

The process starts with students taking the online diagnostic assessment. This online diagnostic test will help assess students' proficiency levels in various standards.

After completion of the diagnostic assessment, students can take note of standards where they are not proficient. This step will help parents and educators in developing a targeted remedial study plan based on a student's proficiency gaps.

Once the targeted remedial study plan is in place, students can start practicing the lessons in this workbook that are focused on specific standards.

After the student completes the targeted remedial practice, the student should attempt the second online STAAR practice test. Record the proficiency levels in the second practice test to measure the student progress and identify any additional learning gaps. Further targeted practice can be planned to help students gain comprehensive skills mastery needed to ensure success on the state assessment.

Lumos Smart Test Prep Methodology

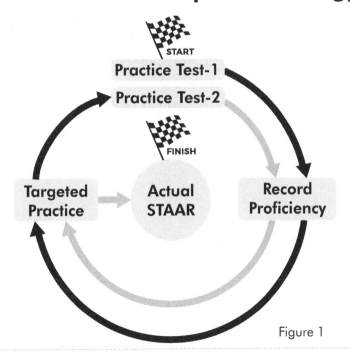

Figure 1

Table of Contents

Sign Up Online

STAAR

Grade 7 Math Practice

Unlock Digital Access

2 STAAR Practice Tests

4 Math Domains

Sign Up Now

Url: https://LumosLearning/a/tedbooks

Access Code: G7MSTAAR-94056-P

Access STAAR Test Practice Resources On Your Mobile Device

Online Access

for

STAAR Practice

+

Printed Workbook

for

Skills Practice

Download Lumos StepUp App
from Google Play Store or Apple App Store

After installing the StepUp App, scan this **QR Code** via **tedBook** section of the mobile app

Chapter 1
Lumos Smart Test Prep Methodology

Step 1: Access Online STAAR Practice Test

The online STAAR practice tests mirror the actual State of Texas Assessment of Academic Readiness in the number of questions, item types, test duration, test tools, and more.

After completing the test, your student will receive immediate feedback with detailed reports on standards mastery and a personalized study plan to overcome any learning gaps. With this study plan, use the next section of the workbook to practice.

Use the URL and access code provided below or scan the QR code to access the first STAAR practice test to get started.

URL	QR Code
Visit the URL below and place the book access code **http://www.lumoslearning.com/a/tedbooks** **Access Code: G7MSTAAR-94056-P**	

Step 2: Review the Personalized Study Plan Online

After students complete the online Practice Test 1, they can access their individualized study plan from the table of contents (Figure 2) Parents and Teachers can also review the study plan through their Lumos account (parent or teacher) portal.

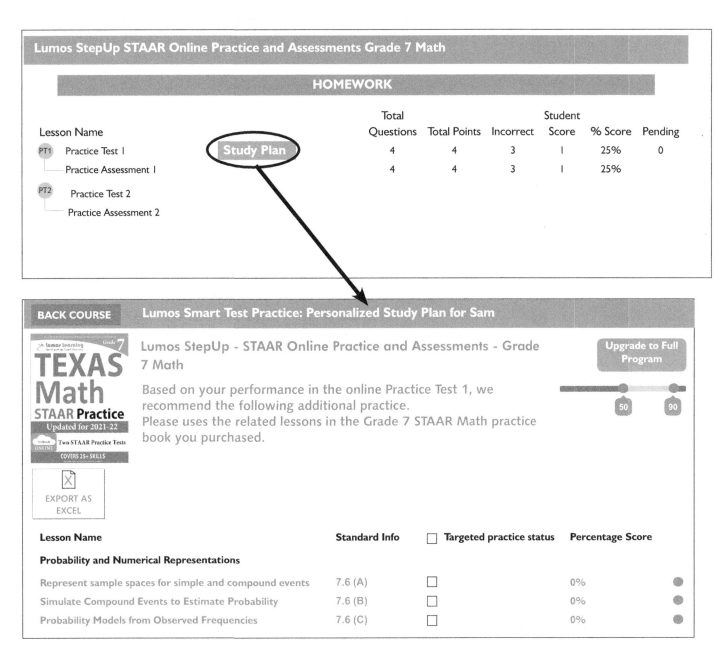

Figure 2

Step 3: Complete Targeted Practice

Using the information provided in the study plan report, complete the targeted practice using the appropriate lessons to overcome proficiency gaps. With lesson names included in the study plan, find the appropriate topics in this workbook and answer the questions provided. Students can refer to the answer key and detailed answers provided for each lesson to gain further understanding of the learning objective. Marking the completed lessons in the study plan after each practice session is recommended.(See Figure 3)

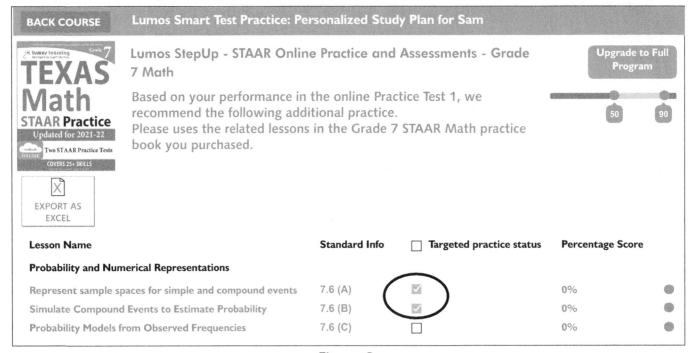

Figure 3

Step 4: Access the Practice Test 2 Online

After completing the targeted practice in this workbook, students should attempt the second STAAR practice test online. Using the student login name and password, login to the Lumos website to complete the second practice test.

Step 5: Repeat Targeted Practice

Repeat the targeted practice as per Step 3 using the second study plan report for Practice test 2 after completion of the second STAAR rehearsal.

Visit http://www.lumoslearning.com/a/lstp for more information on Lumos Smart Test Prep Methodology or Scan the QR Code

Test Taking Tips

1) **The day before the test,** make sure you get a good night's sleep.

2) **On the day of the test,** be sure to eat a good hearty breakfast! Also, be sure to arrive at school on time.

3) **During the test:**

- **Read every question carefully.**

  - Do not spend too much time on any one question. Work steadily through all questions in the section.
  - Attempt all of the questions even if you are not sure of some answers.
  - If you run into a difficult question, eliminate as many choices as you can and then pick the best one from the remaining choices. Intelligent guessing will help you increase your score.
  - Also, mark the question so that if you have extra time, you can return to it after you reach the end of the section.
  - Some questions may refer to a graph, chart, or other kind of picture. Carefully review the graphic before answering the question.
  - Be sure to include explanations for your written responses and show all work.

- **While Answering Multiple-Choice questions.**

  - Read the question completely.
  - Go through the answer choices.
  - If you are struggling with picking out a correct answer, it is best to eliminate some of the choices. At least try to eliminate two of the choices.
  - Reread the question and find support from the passage to support one of the answers.
  - Recheck the question and your answer.

Note: The Texas STAAR Math assessments also includes Grid In type questions in the pencil and paper version of the test.

1ST   2ND
JD S C
JS D C
JC S D
SC S D
DC JS
DS JC

Chapter 2

Probability and Numerical Representations

1 2, 3, 4

Chapter 2

Lesson 1: Represent sample spaces for simple and compound events

1. The triple jump competition is close. Joe, Damon, Sam, and Chris have a shot at first place. If two of the four tie for first place and the other two tie for second place, how many ways could they be arranged in the top two spots?

    4 $2 = 2nd$
          $2 = 1st$

    Ⓐ 6 ways ✓
    Ⓑ 2 ways
    Ⓒ 3 ways
    Ⓓ 8 ways

2. Sam is about to flip three coins. What is the probability he will flip all of the coins to heads?

    $\frac{1}{2} \times \frac{1}{2} \times \frac{1}{2} = \frac{1}{8}$

    Ⓐ 1 out of 4
    Ⓑ 1 out of 6
    Ⓒ 1 out of 8 ✓
    Ⓓ 1 out of 2

3. Jona rolls one six-sided die and one four-sided die. What is the probability she will not roll a 2 or a 3 on either die?

    $\frac{4}{6} (1,4,5,6) \times (1,4) \frac{2}{4} = \frac{8}{24} = \frac{1}{3}$

    Ⓐ 2 out of 3
    Ⓑ 1 out of 3
    Ⓒ 1 out of 4
    Ⓓ 3 out of 4

4. Elsie rolled three four-sided dice. What is the probability she will roll one even and two odds?

    even   odd odd
    $(2 \text{ or } 4)$

    $\frac{2}{4} \times \frac{2}{4} \times \frac{2}{4} = \frac{8}{64}$?

    Ⓐ 1 out of 3
    Ⓑ 3 out of 8
    Ⓒ 1 out of 4
    Ⓓ 5 out of 8

    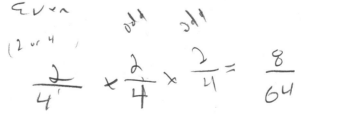

    1,2,34

Name: _____   Date: _____

5. What are the central tendencies of the following data set? (round to the nearest tenth)

    {21, 21, 22, 23, 25, 27, 28, 31, 34, 34, 34, 37}

    Ⓐ Mean: 28.1, Median: 27.5, Mode: 34
    Ⓑ Mean: 28.5, Median: 26, Mode: none
    Ⓒ Mean: 27.5, Median: 28, Mode: none
    Ⓓ Mean: 27, Median: 27.5, Mode: none

6. There are three colors of stones in a bag: red, green, and blue. Two stones are drawn out at random (one at a time). What are the possible outcomes in which exactly one blue stone might be drawn?

    Red, Green, blue

    Ⓐ BR, GB BG
    Ⓑ BG, BR, BB
    Ⓒ RB, GB, BR, BG
    Ⓓ BG, BR

    R B   BG
    G B
    B R

7. A box contains both red checkers and black checkers. Four checkers are drawn out (one at a time). How many different possible outcomes would result in exactly three checkers being red?

    B R R R
    R B R R
    R R B R
    R R R B

    Ⓐ 8
    Ⓑ 2
    Ⓒ 6
    Ⓓ 4

8. A number between 1 and 10 (including 1 and 10) is chosen twice. How many different ways might the same number be chosen both times?

    Ⓐ 5
    Ⓑ 10
    Ⓒ 0
    Ⓓ 3

    1,1
    2,2
    3,3
    4,4 → 10,10

9. A number is chosen between 1 and 10 (including 1 and 10) twice. In how many different ways can you get an even number followed by a prime number?

    Ⓐ 20
    Ⓑ 9
    Ⓒ 25
    Ⓓ 12

    2   1
    4   3
    6   5
    8
    10   7
    ―――
    5   × 4 = 20

10. Two six-side dice are rolled. How many different outcomes for the two dice would result in a total of 7 being rolled?

    Ⓐ 10
    Ⓑ 8
    Ⓒ 6
    Ⓓ 11

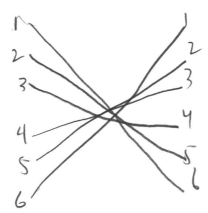

Chapter 2

Lesson 2: Simulate Compound Events to Estimate Probability

1. If 20% of applicants for a job are female, what is the probability that the first two applicants will be male?

   Ⓐ 64%
   Ⓑ 80%
   Ⓒ 60%
   Ⓓ 52%

2. If you want to simulate a random selection from a large population that is 40% adult and 60% children, how can you use slips of paper to do so?

   Ⓐ Make 5 slips of paper, 2 for adults and 3 for children. Randomly select slips of paper from the 5 to represent the choice of someone from the population.
   Ⓑ Make 2 slips of paper, 1 for adults and 1 for children. Randomly select slips of paper from the 2 to represent the choice of someone from the population.
   Ⓒ Make 100 slips of paper, 50 for adults and 50 for children. Randomly select slips of paper from the 100 to represent the choice of someone from the population.
   Ⓓ Make 3 slips of paper, 1 for adults and 2 for children. Randomly select slips of paper from the 3 to represent the choice of someone from the population.

3. A sandwich shop has 6 breads and 5 meats available for sandwiches. What is the probability that two people in a row will choose the same bread and meat combination?

   Ⓐ 1 out of 11
   Ⓑ 1 out of 2
   Ⓒ 1 out of 30
   Ⓓ 1 out of 20

4. A catalogue has sports uniforms for sale. There are 6 designs of shorts that can be combined with 4 designs of shirts. What is the probability that two teams choose different shorts and different shirts?

   Ⓐ 1 out of 2
   Ⓑ 5 out of 8
   Ⓒ 1 out of 4
   Ⓓ 2 out of 7

5. Sally has to choose a pair of pants and a pair of shoes to wear to her club meeting. She can't remember what she wore last time. She has 3 pairs of pants and 5 pairs of shoes to choose from. What is the probability that she will wear the same combination that she wore last time?

   Ⓐ 1 out of 15
   Ⓑ 1 out of 8
   Ⓒ 2 out of 11
   Ⓓ 1 out of 125

6. Suppose that each of the next 5 days there is a 50% chance of rain. You want to know the likelihood of it not raining at all in those 5 days. How can you test that probability with a coin?

   Ⓐ Flip the coin. If it is heads, there will be no rain, and if it is tails, there will be rain. Flip it at least 10 times and see how many times no rain is the result.
   Ⓑ Flip a coin until you get tails, which will represent rain. If you get rain in fewer than 5 coin flips, it will rain in the next five days.
   Ⓒ Flip a coin five times in a row. Repeat this numerous times. Let heads represent no rain and tales represent rain. See how often the five coin flips result in no rain.
   Ⓓ Flip a coin five times. Take the number of times that tails is flipped, and divide it by five. That will tell you the probability of rain in the next five days.

7. Your lawnmower starts well four times out of five. If you have to mow the lawn three more times this season, what is the probability that it will start well all three times?

   Ⓐ About 51%
   Ⓑ About 43%
   Ⓒ About 87%
   Ⓓ About 22%

8. Evan works with his friend Luke. His friend is a good worker, but he has a tendency to be late to work too often. He only shows up on time about 50% of the time. He has already been late once in the first two days of the work week. What is the probability that he will be on time for the remaining three days of the workweek?

   Ⓐ 1 in 5
   Ⓑ 1 in 2
   Ⓒ 1 in 8
   Ⓓ 1 in 6

9. A group of three friends was curious about which day of the week each of them was born on. They decided to research it to find out. What is the probability that all three of them were born on the same day of the week?

    Ⓐ 1 out of 7
    Ⓑ 1 out of 49
    Ⓒ 1 out of 343
    Ⓓ 1 out of 21

10. Two friends both happened to buy new trucks from the same manufacturer in the same week. The manufacturer offers 4 models of trucks in 6 different colors. What is the probability that the two friends happened to buy the same model and color of truck?

    Ⓐ 1 out of 10
    Ⓑ 1 out of 14
    Ⓒ 1 out of 15
    Ⓓ 1 out of 24

Chapter 2

Lesson 3: Probability Models from Observed Frequencies

1. Felix flipped a coin 8 times and got the following results: H, H, T, H, H, T, T, H. If these results were typical for that coin, what are the odds of flipping a heads with that coin?

   Ⓐ 3 out of 5
   Ⓑ 5 out of 8
   Ⓒ 3 out of 8
   Ⓓ 1 out of 2

2. Bridgette rolled a six-sided die 100 times to test the frequency of each number's appearing. According to these statistics, how many times should a 2 be rolled out of 50 rolls?

Number	Frequency
1	18%
2	20%
3	16%
4	11%
5	18%
6	17%

   Ⓐ 10 times
   Ⓑ 20 times
   Ⓒ 12 times
   Ⓓ 15 times

3. Randomly choosing a number out of a hat 50 times resulted in choosing an odd number a total of four more times than the number of times an even number was chosen. How many times was an even number chosen from the hat?

   Ⓐ 27 times
   Ⓑ 21 times
   Ⓒ 29 times
   Ⓓ 23 times

4. 8 out of the last 12 customers at Paul's Pizza ordered pepperoni pizza. According to this data, what is the probability that the next customer will NOT order pepperoni pizza?

   Ⓐ 1 out of 3
   Ⓑ 4 out of 5
   Ⓒ 1 out of 2
   Ⓓ 2 out of 5

5. Susan is selling cookies for a fundraiser. Out of the last 20 people she asked, 10 people bought 1 box of cookies, 5 bought more than 1 box, and 5 bought none. Based on this data, what is the probability that the next person she asks will buy at least 1 box of cookies?

   Ⓐ 1 out of 3
   Ⓑ 2 out of 5
   Ⓒ 4 out of 5
   Ⓓ 3 out of 4

6. William has passed 9 out of his last 10 tests in Spanish class. Based on his past history, what is the probability that he will NOT pass the next test?

   Ⓐ 10%
   Ⓑ 25%
   Ⓒ 15%
   Ⓓ 8%

7. Travis has scored goals in 7 of his last 9 soccer games. At this rate, what is the probability that he will score in his next game? Round the nearest percent.

   Ⓐ 70%
   Ⓑ 17%
   Ⓒ 78%
   Ⓓ 53%

8. Gabe's free throw percentage for the season has been 80%. Based on this, if he has 5 free throws in the next game, how many is he likely to miss?

   Ⓐ 0
   Ⓑ 1
   Ⓒ 2
   Ⓓ 3

9. York and his partner have won the doubles tennis tournament three out of the last four years. According to this record, what is the probability they will win it again this year?

   Ⓐ 3 out of 4
   Ⓑ 1 out of 3
   Ⓒ 1 out of 2
   Ⓓ 4 out of 5

10. Robbie runs track. His finishes for his last 6 events were: 1st, 3rd, 2nd, 5th, 4th, 2nd. Based on these results, what is the probability he will finish in the top 3 of his next event?

    Ⓐ 4 out of 5
    Ⓑ 2 out of 3
    Ⓒ 1 out of 2
    Ⓓ 3 out of 4

Chapter 2

Lesson 4: Using Probability Models

1. Sara rolls two dice, one black and one yellow. What is the probability that she will roll a 3 on the black die and a 5 on the yellow die?

   Ⓐ $\dfrac{1}{6}$

   Ⓑ $\dfrac{1}{12}$

   Ⓒ $\dfrac{2}{15}$

   Ⓓ $\dfrac{1}{36}$

2. Which of the following represents the probability of an event most likely to occur?

   Ⓐ   0.25
   Ⓑ   0.91
   Ⓒ   0.58
   Ⓓ   0.15

3. Which of the following is not a valid probability?

   Ⓐ   0.25

   Ⓑ $\dfrac{1}{5}$

   Ⓒ   1

   Ⓓ $\dfrac{5}{4}$

4. Joe has 5 nickels, 5 dimes, 5 quarters, and 5 pennies in his pocket. Six times, he randomly picked a coin from his pocket and put it back. Joe picked a dime every time. If he randomly picks a coin from his pocket again, what is the probability the coin will be a dime?

Ⓐ 33%
Ⓑ 100%
Ⓒ 24%
Ⓓ 25%

5. Jim rolls a pair of six-sided dice five times. He rolls a pair of two's five times in a row. If he rolls the dice one more time, what is the probability he will roll a pair of fours?

Ⓐ 1 out of 21
Ⓑ 1 out of 36
Ⓒ 1 out of 24
Ⓓ 1 out of 6

6. Bob rolls a six-sided die and flips a coin five times. He rolls a three and flips the coin to tails five times in a row. If he rolls the die and flips the coin one more time, what is the probability he will roll a three and flip the coin on tails?

Ⓐ 1 out of 6
Ⓑ 1 out of 10
Ⓒ 1 out of 12
Ⓓ 1 out of 7

7. Mia rolls a pair of six-sided dice and flips two coins ten times. She rolls a pair of threes and flips the coins to tails ten times in a row. If she rolls the dice and flips the coins one more time, what is the probability she will roll all fives and flip the coins on heads?

Ⓐ 1 out of 60
Ⓑ 1 out of 144
Ⓒ 1 out of 128
Ⓓ 1 out of 64

8. Sophia wants to select a pair of shorts from Too Sweet Clothing Store. The store has 2 different colors of shorts (black (B) and green (G)) available in sizes of small (S), medium (M), and large (L). If Sophia grabs a pair of shorts without looking, which sample space shows the different types of shorts she could select?

Ⓐ {BS, BM, BL, GS, GM, GL}
Ⓑ {BB, BG, SS, SM, SL}
Ⓒ {BG, SM, SL}
Ⓓ {BS, BL, GS, GL}

9. Tom tosses a coin 12 times. The coin lands on heads only twice. If Tom tosses the coin one more time, what is the probability that the coin will land on heads?

Ⓐ 40%
Ⓑ 50%
Ⓒ 60%
Ⓓ 15%

10. Eric's Pizza Shop is offering a sale on any large two-topping pizza for $8.00. Customers have a choice between thin crust (T) or pan pizza (Z), one meat topping [pepperoni(P), Italian sausage (I), or ham (H)], and one vegetable topping [green peppers (G), onions (O), or mushrooms (M)]. Which sample space shows the number of possible combinations customers can have if they select a thin crust pizza?

Ⓐ {TPG, TIO, THM}
Ⓑ {TPG, TPO, TPM, TIG, TIO, TIM, THG, THO, THM}
Ⓒ {TPG, TPO, TIG, TIO, THG, THO}
Ⓓ {TPG, TPO, TPM, TIG, TIO, TIM, THG, THO, THM, PPG, PPO, PPM, PIG, PIO, PIM, PHG, PHO, PHM}

Chapter 2

Lesson 5: Problems using central tendency

1. **Bella recorded the number of newspapers left over at the end of each day for a week. What is the average number of newspapers left each day?**

   3, 6, 1, 0, 2, 3, 6

   Ⓐ 2 newspapers
   Ⓑ 3 newspapers
   Ⓒ 4.3 newspapers
   Ⓓ 6 newspapers

2. **Recorded below are the ages of eight friends. Which statement is true about this data set?**

   13, 18, 14, 12, 15, 19, 11, 15

   Ⓐ Mean > Median > Mode
   Ⓑ Mode < Mean < Median
   Ⓒ Median > Mode < Median
   Ⓓ Mode > Mean > Median

3. **The line plot below represents the high temperature in °F each day of a rafting trip. What was the average high temperature during the trip?**

   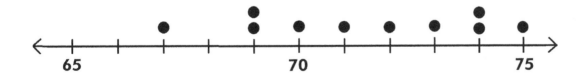

   Ⓐ 70°F
   Ⓑ 71°F
   Ⓒ 71.4°F
   Ⓓ 72°F

4. **What is the mean absolute deviation of the grades Charlene received on her first ten quizzes: 83%, 92%, 76%, 87%, 89%, 96%, 88%, 91%, 79%, 99%.**

   Ⓐ 4.5%
   Ⓑ 5.4%
   Ⓒ 88%
   Ⓓ 88.5%

5. **The following numbers are the minutes it took Nyak to complete one lap around a certain dirt bike course. What is the mean absolute deviation of this data set?**

   12.3, 12.6, 12.2, 10.9, 11.3, 10.3, 11.7, 10.7

   Ⓐ 0.7 minutes
   Ⓑ 0.75 minutes
   Ⓒ 11.1 minutes
   Ⓓ 1.5 minutes

6. **The local Akita Rescue Organization has nine Akitas for adoption. Their weights are 82 lbs, 95, lbs, 130 lbs, 112 lbs, 122 lbs, 72 lbs, 86, lbs, 145 lbs, 93 lbs. What are the median (M), 1st Quartile (Q1), 3rd Quartile (Q3) and Interquartile Range (IQR) of this data set?**

   Ⓐ M = 95, Q1 = 84, Q3 = 126, IQR = 42
   Ⓑ M = 95, Q1 = 85, Q3 = 126, IQR = 145
   Ⓒ M = 95, Q1 = 84, Q3 = 145, IQR = 42
   Ⓓ M = 95, Q1 = 126, Q3 = 145, IQR = 42

7. **Monica is keeping track of how much money she spends on lunch each school day. This week Monica spent $5.20, $6.50, $3.75, $0.75, and $4.15. What is the median (M) and Interquartile Range (IQR) of Monica's lunch expenese?**

   Ⓐ M = $4.15, IQR = $1.45
   Ⓑ M = $4.07, IQR = $1.45
   Ⓒ M = $4.07, IQR = $2.25
   Ⓓ M = $4.15, IQR = $3.60

8. **Monica's friend Anna is also tracking her school lunch expenses. This week Anna spent $2.60, $0, $7.00, $4.40, $3.75. What is the difference between Monica's and Anna's average daily lunch expense?**

   Monica: $5.20, $6.50, $3.75, $0.75, and $4.15

   Ⓐ $0.40
   Ⓑ $0.52
   Ⓒ $0.60
   Ⓓ $1.50

9. Zahra and Tyland are very competitive. Each have recorded their basketball scores since the beginning of the season. Which data set has a greater Interquartile Range (IQR)?

Name	Scores
Zahra	8, 10, 3, 12, 14, 11
Tyland	6, 7, 18, 12, 4, 9

Ⓐ Zahra has the higher IQR of 4.
Ⓑ Zahra has the higher IQR of 10.5.
Ⓒ Tyland's IQR is 2 points higher than Zahra's.
Ⓓ Tyland and Zahra have the same IQR of 5.

10. Jamila records the number of customers she gets each day for a week: 20, 42, 15, 23, 53, 62, 58. What is the mean absolute deviation of this data?

Ⓐ 16.9 customers
Ⓑ 19 customers
Ⓒ 39 customers
Ⓓ 47.5 customers

Chapter 2

Lesson 6: Determine experimental and theoretical probabilities

1. **Which of the following represents the sample space for flipping two coins?**

   Ⓐ {HH, TT}
   Ⓑ {H, T}
   Ⓒ {HH, HT, TH, TT}
   Ⓓ {HH, HT, TT}

2. **Which of the following experiments would best test the statement, "The probability of a coin landing on heads is 1/2."?**

   Ⓐ Toss a coin 1,000 times, and record the results.
   Ⓑ Toss a coin twice to see if it lands on heads one out of those two times.
   Ⓒ Toss a coin until it lands on heads and record the number of tries it took.
   Ⓓ Toss a coin twice, if it doesn't land on heads exactly once, the theoretical probability is false.

3. **Which of the following results is most likely from rolling a six-sided die?**

   Ⓐ Rolling an odd number
   Ⓑ Rolling an even number
   Ⓒ Rolling a number from 1 to 3
   Ⓓ All of the above are equally likely.

4. **Sandy flipped a coin 40 times. Her results are 75% heads and 25% tails. What is the difference between the actual results and the expected results of flipping heads?**

   Ⓐ 20%
   Ⓑ 50%
   Ⓒ 25%
   Ⓓ 10%

5. Maggie rolled a pair of four sided dice 10 times. The results are 30% side 1, 20% side 2, 20% side 3, 30% side 4. What is the difference between the results and the expected results for all four sides?

Ⓐ 25% side 1,
     25% side 2,
     25% side 3,
     25% side 4

Ⓑ 5% side 1,
     5% side 2,
     5% side 3,
     5% side 4

Ⓒ 5% side 1,
     25% side 2,
     25% side 3,
     5% side 4

Ⓓ 4% side 1,
     4% side 2,
     4% side 3,
     4% side 4

6. Moe has a bowl of nuts (14 pecans, 8 walnuts, 28 almonds, 33 peanuts). If he picks a nut at random, what is the probability that he will pick a peanut?

Ⓐ 33 out of 70
Ⓑ 33 out of 80
Ⓒ 33 out of 100
Ⓓ 33 out of 83

7. Xavier has a bowl of nuts (14 pecans, 8 walnuts, 28 almonds, 33 peanuts). If he picks out all the pecans, what is the probability that he will pick a walnut at random?

Ⓐ 8 out of 83
Ⓑ 8 out of 69
Ⓒ 8 out of 100
Ⓓ 8 out of 70

8. Tim has a box of chocolates with the following flavors: 24 cherry, 26 caramel, 20 fudge, and 16 candy. If he picks out two of each type of chocolate, what is the probability that he will pick a cherry chocolate at random?

    Ⓐ 11 out of 35
    Ⓑ 4 out of 13
    Ⓒ 11 out of 50
    Ⓓ 11 out of 39

9. Clarissa has a box of chocolates with the following flavors: 24 cherry, 26 caramel, 20 fudge, and 16 taffy. If she picks out all the taffy, what is the probability that she will pick a fudge chocolate at random?

    Ⓐ 2 out of 7
    Ⓑ 10 out of 43
    Ⓒ 1 out of 5
    Ⓓ 8 out of 35

10. Karen has a box of chocolates with the following flavors: 24 cherry, 26 caramel, 20 fudge, and 16 taffy. If she removes half of the cherry and fudge chocolates from the box, what is the probability that she will pick a taffy chocolate at random?

    Ⓐ 1 out of 4
    Ⓑ 8 out of 43
    Ⓒ 4 out of 25
    Ⓓ 16 out of 43

End of Probability and Numerical Representations

Answer Key and Detailed Explanations

Chapter 2: Numerical Representations and Relationships

Lesson 1: Represent sample spaces for simple and compound events

Question No.	Answer	Detailed Explanations
1	A	There are 6 ways to arrange the players for the top two spots (combining duplicates): JDSC, JCDS, SCDJ, SJCD, CDSJ, SDJC.
2	C	For every three coin flips, there are 8 possible outcomes. 1 of those outcomes would contain all heads. So, the probability is 1 out of 8.
3	B	For every roll of a 6-sided die and a 4-sided die, there are 24 possible outcomes. Of these, 16 outcomes contain a 2 or a 3 (or both). This leaves 8 favorable outcomes. So the probability is 8 out of 24, or 1 out of 3.
4	B	For every roll of three 4-sided dice, there are 64 possible outcomes. 24 of these outcomes would contain one even and two odds. Therefore, the probability is 24 out of 64, or 3 out of 8.
5	A	To find the mean, add the numbers together, and divide by the amount of numbers in the data set. (1) 21 + 21 + 22 + 23 + 25 + 27 + 28 + 31 +34 + 34 + 34 + 37 = 337 (2) 337 ÷ 12 = 28.1 To find the median, find the middle number in the data set. One way to find the median is to order the numbers from least to greatest and cross out the numbers until the middle is reached. Here, the middle numbers are 27 and 28. Add the numbers together and divide by 2. (1) 28 + 27 = 55 (2) 55 ÷ 2 = 27.5 To find the mode, find the number that appears most in the data set. Looking at the numbers shows that the number 34 appears 3 times; therefore 34 is the mode.
6	D	The blue stone might be either the first or second of the stones. The other stone could be either red or green.
7	D	If three of the checkers are red, then one is black. The black could be drawn out as the first, second, third, or fourth of the checkers, so there are four ways this could take place.
8	B	The number that is chosen both times could be any of the 10 numbers.
9	A	The first number can be any of the 5 even numbers (2, 4, 6, 8, and 10) and the second number can be any of the 4 prime numbers (2, 3, 5, and 7). Therefore, there are 5 x 4 = 20 different ways of getting an even number followed by a prime number.
10	C	The sample space for this outcome would be: (1, 6), (2, 5), (3, 4), (4, 3), (5, 2), and (6, 1). There are six possible outcomes.

Lesson 2: Simulate Compound Events to Estimate Probability

Question No.	Answer	Detailed Explanations
1	A	The probability of the first applicant is male = 1-0.20 = 0.80, another applicant is also a male = 0.80. So, the probability is 0.80*0.80 = 0.64*100 = 64%
2	A	The slips of paper should be in the same ratio as the population, which can be done by 2 adult slips and 3 child slips.
3	C	The probability that the second customer will choose the same bread as the first is 1 in 6. The probability that he will choose the same meat is 1 in 5. Multiply these together to find the probability of choosing both.
4	B	The probability of choosing different shorts is 5 out of 6. The probability of choosing different shirts is 3 out of 4. Multiplying these together to find the probability of both gives us 5 out of 8.
5	A	The probability of choosing the same pants is 1 in 3. The probability of choosing the same shoes is 1 in 5. Multiply these together to get the probability of the same combination of both, which is 1 in 15.
6	C	You must get 5 consecutive flips without rain to represent five days without rain. You must also test this numerous times and record the percentage of the time that no rain is the result.
7	A	The probability of it starting well one time is four out of five. You must multiply this together three times, though, to find the probability of it starting well all three times that you have to mow. The result is about 51%.
8	C	He has a 1 in 2 chance of being on time one day. Multiply this together three times to find the likelihood that he will be on time all three remaining days. The probability is 1 in 8.
9	C	The first friend could be born on any of the seven days of the week. The probability that the second friend was born on the same day as the first is 1 in 7. The probability that the third was born on that same day is also 1 in 7. Multiply these probabilities together to find the probability that they were all born on the same day. 1/7 * 1/7 * 1/7 = 1/343. 1 in 343 is the answer.
10	D	After the first person has chosen the truck, the probability that the second person choose the same model is 1 in 4 and he (second person) choose the same color is 1 in 6. Therefore, the probability that the second person choose the same model and same color as the first person = $(\frac{1}{4}) \times (\frac{1}{6}) = \frac{1}{24}$.

Lesson 3: Probability Models from Observed Frequencies

Question No.	Answer	Detailed Explanations
1	B	Because 5 of the 8 times it was flipped, the result was heads, the probability of heads is 5 out of 8.
2	A	If 20% of the rolls result in a 2, then 20% of 50 rolls would be (0.20)(50) = 10 times.
3	D	An even distribution of the odds and evens would be 25 each. 4 more odds would mean 27 odds and 23 evens.
4	A	4 out of 12 customers did NOT order pepperoni. This simplifies to 1 out of 3.
5	D	15 out of the 20 people ordered 1 box or more. This reduces down to 3 out of every 4 people.
6	A	Only 1 time out of 10 did he NOT pass the test, so this is a 10% probability.
7	C	7 out of 9 is a 77.777...% probability, which rounds to 78%.
8	B	An 80% success rate means that he makes 4 out of 5 and misses only 1 out of every 5 free throws.
9	A	The fact that 3 of the last 4 years they won the tournament suggests that this year's probability of winning is that same 3 out of 4.
10	B	4 out of the last 6 results were in the top three, so this simplifies to a 2 out of 3 probability.

Lesson 4: Using Probability Models

Question No.	Answer	Detailed Explanations
1	D	Remember: In a compound and event, you can multiply the probabilities of each event in order to arrive at a final solution. There is a $\frac{1}{6}$ chance she will roll a 3 and a $\frac{1}{6}$ chance Sara rolls a 5. This means there is a $\frac{1}{6}(\frac{1}{6}) = \frac{1}{36}$ chance she will roll both. Another way to approach this problem is to create the sample space containing all possible combinations. (B, Y): (1,1), (1,2), (1,3), (1,4), (1,5), (1,6) (2,1), (2,2), (2,3), (2,4), (2,5), (2,6) (3,1), (3,2), (3,3), (3,4), (3,5), (3,6) (4,1), (4,2), (4,3), (4,4), (4,5), (4,6) (5,1), (5,2), (5,3), (5,4), (5,5), (5,6) (6,1), (6,2), (6,3), (6,4), (6,5), (6,6) From this list it is clear that only one out of the 36 total possible matches the (3,5) described.
2	B	Probability is defined as chance that an event will occur (a number between 0 and 1). The closer a probability is to 1, the more likely it is to occur. Drawing a number line with marks 0.1 distance apart can help determine the likelihood of an event occurring. Since 0.91 is close to 1, it represents an event most likely to occur.
3	D	Probability is defined as the chance that an event will occur (a number from 0 to 1). Since $\frac{5}{4}$ is a rational number greater than 1, it cannot represent a probability.
4	D	Since there are the same amount of coins in each amount, the theoretical probability (expected outcome) of picking a coin is 1 out of 4 because Joe will either pick a penny, a nickel, a dime or a quarter. 1 out of 4 is equivalent to 25%.
5	B	For every roll of two 6-sided dice, there are 36 possible outcomes. Therefore, the probability of rolling a pair of fours is 1 out of 36.
6	C	For every roll of a 6-sided die and coin flip, there are 12 possible outcomes: {(1,h), (1,t), (2,h), (2,t), (3,h), (3,t), (4,h), (4,t), (5,h), (5,t), (6,h), (6,t)}. Therefore, the possibility of rolling a three and flipping tails is 1 out of 12.
7	B	For every roll of two 6-sided dice and two coin flips, there are 144 possible outcomes (36 x 4). Therefore, the probability of rolling two fives and flipping two heads is 1 out of 144.
8	A	The sample space of {BS, BM, BL, GS, GM, GL} is the correct answer. Since Sophia has a choice of 2 different pairs of shorts in 3 different combinations, the sample space should reflect choices of black or green shorts in sizes of small, medium, or large.

Question No.	Answer	Detailed Explanations
9	B	Theoretical probability is the (number of possible favorable outcomes)/(total number of outcomes). Each time Tom flips a coin, there is 1 possible favorable outcome (heads) out of 2 total possible outcomes. Therefore, the probability is $\frac{1}{2}$, which is equivalent to 50%.
10	B	For each type of crust, there are 9 possible combinations. Therefore, the sample space {TPG, TPO, TPM, TIG, TIO, TIM, THG, THO, THM} represents the number of combinations if a customer chooses a thin crust pizza.

Lesson 5: Problems using central tendency

Question No.	Answer	Detailed Explanations
1	B	Find the total number of newspapers leftover and divide by the number of days. $$\frac{3+6+1+0+2+3+6}{7} = \frac{21}{7} = 3 \text{ newspapers}$$
2	D	Find the mean, median, and mode of the data set and compare. Mean: $$\frac{13+18+14+12+15+19+11+15}{8} = \frac{117}{8} = 14.625$$ Median: 11, 12, 13, 14, 15, 15, 18, 19 → 14.5 Mode: 15 Mode > Mean > Median
3	C	Add the temperatures and divide by the number of temperatures. $$\frac{67+69+69+70+71+72+73+74+74+75}{10} = \frac{714}{10} = 71.4°F$$
4	B	First find the mean. $$\frac{83+92+76+87+89+96+88+91+79+99}{10} = \frac{880}{10} = 88\%$$ Now find the distance between each number and the average. $\|83-88\|=5$ $\|92-88\|=4$ $\|76-88\|=12$ $\|87-88\|=1$ $\|89-88\|=1$ $\|96-88\|=8$ $\|88-88\|=0$ $\|91-88\|=3$ $\|79-88\|=9$ $\|99-88\|=11$ Take the average of these differences $$\frac{5+4+12+1+1+8+0+3+9+11}{10} = \frac{54}{10} = 5.4\%$$

Question No.	Answer	Detailed Explanations
5	A	First find the mean.

$$\frac{12.3 + 12.6 + 12.2 + 10.9 + 11.3 + 10.3 + 11.7 + 10.7}{8} = \frac{92}{8} = 11.5$$

Now find the distance between each number and the average.

$$|12.3-11.5|=0.8$$
$$|12.6-11.5|=1.1$$
$$|12.2-11.5|=0.7$$
$$|10.9-11.5|=0.6$$
$$|11.3-11.5|=0.2$$
$$|10.3-11.5|=1.2$$
$$|11.7-11.5|=0.2$$
$$|10.7-11.5|=0.8$$

Take the average of these differences

$$\frac{0.8 + 1.1 + 0.7 + 0.6 + 0.2 + 1.2 + 0.2 + 0.8}{8} = \frac{5.6}{8} = 0.7 min$$

Question No.	Answer	Detailed Explanations
6	A	Put the numbers in order from least to greatest.

72 82 86 93 95 112 122 130 145

Median = 95

$$Q1 = \frac{82 + 86}{2} = 84$$

$$Q3 = \frac{122 + 130}{2} = 126$$

IQR = 126 − 84 = 42

M = 95, Q1 = 84, Q3 = 126, IQR = 42

Question No.	Answer	Detailed Explanations
7	D	Put the numbers in order from least to greatest.

$0.75 $3.75 $4.15 $5.20 $6.50

Median = $4.15

$$Q1 = \frac{0.75 + 3.75}{2} = \$2.25$$

$$Q3 = \frac{5.20 + 6.50}{2} = \$5.85$$

IQR = 5.85 - 2.25 = $3.60

M = $4.15, IQR = $3.60

Question No.	Answer	Detailed Explanations
8	B	Find the average of both and then find the difference.

Anna: $\frac{2.60 + 0 + 7.00 + 4.40 + 3.7}{5} = \frac{17.75}{5} = \$3.55$

Monica: $\frac{5.20 + 6.50 + 3.75 + 0.75 + 4.1}{5} = \frac{20.35}{5} = \$4.07$

Difference: $4.07 − $3.55 = $0.52

Question No.	Answer	Detailed Explanations
9	C	Zahra: 3 8 10 11 12 14 Median $= \dfrac{10 + 11}{2} = \dfrac{21}{2} = 10.5$ Q1 = 8 Q3 = 12 IQR = 12 − 8 = 4 Tyland: 4 6 7 9 12 18 Median $= \dfrac{7 + 9}{2} = \dfrac{16}{2} = 8$ Q1 = 6 Q3 = 12 IQR = 12 − 6 = 6 Tyland has the greater IQR of 6, which is 2 points higher tha Zahra's.
10	A	First find the mean. $\dfrac{20 + 42 + 15 + 23 + 53 + 62 + 58}{7} = \dfrac{273}{7} = 39$ Now find the distance between each number and the average. $\|20-39\|=19$ $\|42-39\|=3$ $\|15-39\|=24$ $\|23-39\|=16$ $\|53-39\|=14$ $\|62-39\|=23$ $\|58-39\|=19$ Take the average of these differences $\dfrac{19 + 3 + 24 + 16 + 14 + 23 + 19}{7} = \dfrac{118}{7} = 16.9 \; customers$

Lesson 6: Determine experimental and theoretical probabilities

Question No.	Answer	Detailed Explanations
1	C	Create a sample space by listing all the possible outcomes. For each coin flipped, it will land on heads or tails. Therefore, for two coins, there could be outcomes of (heads, heads), (heads, tails), (tails, heads), and (tails, tails).
2	A	When testing probability, larger samples (experiments) yield more accurate results. An experiment of 1,000 coin tosses could adequately test if a coin would land on its head $\frac{1}{2}$ of the time (about 500 of 1,000).
3	D	Since there are three even numbers (2, 4, 6) and three odd numbers (1, 3, 5) on a six-sided die, the probability is 3 out of 6 for rolling either an even or an odd number. Therefore, it is equally likely to roll an even or odd number. There is also a 3 out of 6 chance of rolling a number from 1 to 3.
4	C	The theoretical probability (expected outcome) of flipping a coin is 1 out of 2 because it will either land on heads or tails (those are the two possible outcomes). 1 out of 2 is equivalent to 50%. Subtract the expected outcome from the actual outcome 75% (75 - 50 = 25) and add the percent sign: 25%
5	B	The theoretical probability (expected outcome) of rolling each die is 1 out of 4 because it will either land on 1, 2, 3 or 4 (those are the four possible outcomes). One out of 4 is equal to 25%. Therefore, the difference between the expected results and the actual results is 5% for each side.
6	D	Moe has a total of 83 nuts, 33 of which are peanuts. Probability is: $\frac{\text{chance of successful outcome}}{\text{total number of outcomes}}$. Therefore, there is a 33 out of 83 chance that Moe will pick a peanut.
7	B	Xavier has a total of 83 nuts, 8 of which are walnuts. If he removes the pecans, he will have 69 nuts remaining (83 - 14 = 69). Probability is: $\frac{\text{chance of successful outcome}}{\text{total number of outcomes}}$. Therefore, there is an 8 out of 69 chance that Xavier will pick a walnut.

Question No.	Answer	Detailed Explanations
8	D	Tim had a total of 86 chocolates. If he removes 2 of each type of chocolate, he will have 22 cherry, 24 caramel, 18 fudge, and 14 candy remaining for a total of 78 chocolates. Probability is: $\dfrac{\text{chance of successful outcome}}{\text{total number of outcomes}}$ Therefore, there is a 22 out of 78 chance that Tim will pick a cherry chocolate. This reduces to 11 out of 39.
9	A	Clarissa had a total of 86 chocolates. If she removes all of the taffy, she will have 70 chocolates remaining. Probability is: $\dfrac{\text{chance of successful outcome}}{\text{total number of outcomes}}$ Therefore, there is a 20 out of 70 chance that Clarissa will pick a fudge chocolate. This reduces to 2 out of 7.
10	A	Karen had a total of 86 chocolates. If she removes $\frac{1}{2}$ of the cherry and fudge chocolates, she will have 12 cherry, 26 caramel, 10 fudge, and 16 taffy remaining for a total of 64 chocolates. Probability is: $\dfrac{\text{chance of successful outcome}}{\text{total number of outcomes}}$. Therefore, there is a 16 out of 64 chance that Karen will pick a taffy chocolate. This reduces to 1 out of 4.

Chapter 3

Computations and Algebraic Relationships

Chapter 3

Lesson 1: Rational Numbers, Multiplication & Division

1. **Convert to a decimal:** $\dfrac{7}{8}$

   Ⓐ 0.78
   Ⓑ 0.81
   ⬤ 0.875
   Ⓓ 0.925

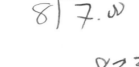

2. **Convert to a decimal:** $\dfrac{5}{6}$

   ⬤ 0.8333333...
   Ⓑ 0.56
   Ⓒ 0.94
   Ⓓ 0.8

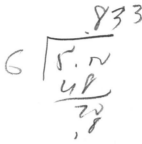

3. How can you tell that the following number is a rational number?

   0.251

   Ⓐ It is a rational number because the decimal terminates. ✓
   Ⓑ It is a rational number because there is a value of 0 in the ones place.
   Ⓒ It is a rational number because the sum of the digits is less than 10.
   Ⓓ It is a rational number because it is not a repeating decimal.

4. **A group of 11 friends ordered 4 pizzas to share. They divided the pizzas up evenly and all ate the same amount. Express in decimal form the portion of a pizza that each friend ate.**

   ⬤ 0.36363636...
   Ⓑ 0.411
   Ⓒ 0.14141414...
   Ⓓ 0.48

5. How can you tell that the following number is a rational number?

   0.133333...

   Ⓐ It is rational because the decimal does not terminate.
   Ⓑ It is rational because the decimal repeats over and over.
   Ⓒ It is rational because the number is a factor of 1.
   ⬤ It is NOT rational because the decimal does not terminate.

6. Fill in the blank to make a true equation.

$(-9)*(\underline{}) = 36$

Ⓐ - 4
Ⓑ 4
Ⓒ 6
Ⓓ - 6

7. Solve for x. $x = 96$

$x = (-2)(6)(-4)$ $9 \times 6 = 2$

Ⓐ x = 36
Ⓑ x = 0
Ⓒ x = 48
Ⓓ x = - 48

8. Which of the following represents the product of 0.53 * 11.6?

Ⓐ 0.6148
Ⓑ 6.148
Ⓒ 61.48
Ⓓ 614.8

9. Which of the following is NOT a rational number?

Ⓐ $\dfrac{8}{15}$

Ⓑ 20.6

Ⓒ $\sqrt{3}$

Ⓓ $\dfrac{9}{11}$

10. Which of the following numbers is divisible by 3?

Ⓐ 459,732
Ⓑ 129,682
Ⓒ 1,999,000
Ⓓ 5,684,722

Chapter 3

Lesson 2: Apply and extend previous understanding of operations to solve problems

1. Andrew has $9.39 but needs $15.00 to make a purchase. How much more does he need?

$15 - 9.39$

Ⓐ $6.39
● $5.61
Ⓒ $5.39
Ⓓ $6.61

2. Ben has to unload a truck filled with 25 bags of grain for his horses. Each bag weighs 50.75 pounds.

How many total pounds does he have to move?

25×50.70

Ⓐ 12,687.50 pounds
● 1,268.75 pounds
Ⓒ 126.875 pounds
Ⓓ 1250 pounds

3. A Chinese restaurant purchased 1528.80 pounds of rice. If they received 50 identical bags, how much rice was in each bag?

● 30.576 pounds
Ⓑ 305.76 pounds
Ⓒ 3.0576 pounds
Ⓓ None of the above.

$$50\overline{)1528.80} \quad 30.576$$

150
280
250 380

50
×4
200

4. John had $76.00. He gave Jim $42.45 and gave Todd $21.34. John will receive $14.50 later in the evening. How much money will John have later that night?

Ⓐ $25.71
Ⓑ $26.67
● $26.71
Ⓓ $24.71

```
  76.86
- 42.45
  33.55
- 21.34
  12.21
+ 14.50
  26.71
```

5. Evaluate: 25 + 2.005 - 7.253 - 2.977

Ⓐ -16.775
● 16.775
Ⓒ 167.75
Ⓓ 1.6775

```
  27.005
-  7.253
  19.752
-  2.977
  15.775
```

6. Mickey bought pizza and sodas for himself and four of his friends. The pizza was $17.49, and 5 sodas were $1.19 each.

   If the pizza is sliced into 10 equal slices and each person eats 2 slices and drinks one soda, what is the cost to each person?

   Ⓐ $2.94
   Ⓑ $4.13
   Ⓒ $3.50
   Ⓓ $4.69

   (handwritten: $1.19   17.49   159.95 = 109.24   5 89.68)

7. Ricky purchased shoes for $159.95 and then exchanged them at a buy 1, get 1 half off sale. The shoes that he purchased on his return trip were $74.99 and $68.55. How much did he receive back from the store after his second transaction?

   Ⓐ $37.50
   Ⓑ $68.55
   Ⓒ $34.28
   Ⓓ $50.68

   (handwritten: 74.99 + 34.28 = (109.27)   174.99 + 68.55 = 143.54   68.55   51.40)

8. Simplify the following expression:

   $$3.24 - 1.914 - 6.025 + 9.86 - 2.2 + 5\frac{1}{2} =$$

   Ⓐ -8.461
   Ⓑ 8.461
   Ⓒ -11.259
   Ⓓ 11.259

   (handwritten: 23.240 = 1.914   1.326   -8.825 - 1.326 -4.699   9.880 -4.699   45.161   21.200   12.961 +5.500   8.461 / 2)

9. Leila stopped at the coffee shop on her way to work. She ordered 2 bagels, 3 yogurts, and 1 orange juice. Bagels were $0.69 each, yogurts were $1.49 each, and orange juice was $1.75. What was Leila's total bill?

   Ⓐ $7.60
   Ⓑ $3.93
   Ⓒ $5.16
   Ⓓ $5.42

   (handwritten: 0.67 + 0.69 = 1.38   1.49 × 3 = 4.47   1.38 + 4.47 = 5.85 + 1.75 = 7.60)

10. Jeri has had a savings account since she entered first grade. Each month of the first year she saved $1.00. Each month of the second year she saved $2.00 etc until she completed ten years in which she saved $10.00 each month. How much does she have saved at the end of ten years?

    Ⓐ $660
    Ⓑ $648
    Ⓒ $636
    Ⓓ $624

    (handwritten: 1×12=12   2×12=24   3×12=36   4×12=48   5×12   12 ×10 00 +12 120   240   12 10   12 ×5   240)

Chapter 3

Lesson 3: Represent proportions by equations

1. 3 hats cost a total of $18. Which equation describes the total cost, C, in terms of the number of hats, n?

    Ⓐ C = 3n
    Ⓑ C = 6n
    Ⓒ C = 0.5n
    Ⓓ 3C = n

2. Use the data in the table to give an equation to represent the proportional relationship.

x	y
0.5	7
1	14
1.5	21
2	28

    Ⓐ y = 14x
    Ⓑ y = 7x
    Ⓒ 7y = x
    Ⓓ 21y = x

3. Kelli has purchased a membership at the gym for the last four months. She has paid the same amount each month, and her total cost so far has been $100. What equation expresses the proportional relationship of the cost and month?

    Ⓐ C = 100m
    Ⓑ C = 50m
    Ⓒ C = 4m
    Ⓓ C = 25m

4. When buying bananas at the market, Marco pays $4.50 for 5 pounds. What is the relationship between pounds, p, and cost, C?

    Ⓐ C = 4.5p
    Ⓑ C = 5p
    Ⓒ C = 0.9p
    Ⓓ C = 22.5p

5. The cost to rent an apartment is proportional to the number of square feet in the apartment. An 800 square foot apartment costs $600 per month. What equation represents the relationship between area, a, and cost, C?

Ⓐ C = 0.75a
Ⓑ C = 1.33a
Ⓒ C = 8a
Ⓓ C = 6a

6. A school has to purchase new desks for their classrooms. They have to purchase 350 new desks, and they pay $7000. What equation demonstrates the relationship between the number of desks, d, and the total cost, C?

Ⓐ C = 10d
Ⓑ C = 20d
Ⓒ C = 70d
Ⓓ C = 35d

7. A soccer club is hosting a tournament with 12 teams involved. Each team has a set number of players, and there are a total of 180 players involved in the tournament. Which equation represents the proportional relationship between teams, t, and players, p?

Ⓐ p = 15t
Ⓑ p = 12t
Ⓒ p = 18t
Ⓓ p = 11t

8. A package of three rolls of tape costs $5 per pack. What is the proportional relationship between cost, C, and package of tape, p?

Ⓐ C = 1.67p
Ⓑ C = 15p
Ⓒ C = 3p
Ⓓ C = 5p

9. Freddy is building a house and has 5 loads of gravel delivered for the work. His total cost for the gravel is $1750. Which equation correctly shows the relationship between cost, C, and loads of gravel, g?

Ⓐ C = 5g
Ⓑ C = 350g
Ⓒ C = 75g
Ⓓ C = 225g

10. Use the graph to write an equation for the proportional relationship between the number of hours Corrie works, h, and her total pay, P.

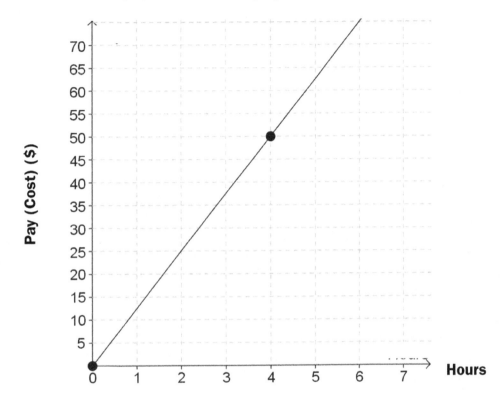

Ⓐ   P = 12.50h
Ⓑ   P = 50h
Ⓒ   P = 4h
Ⓓ   P = 22.50h

Chapter 3

Lesson 4: Unit Rates

1. A tennis match was delayed because of rain. The officials were not prepared for the delay. They covered the 25ft by 20ft court with 13ft by 10ft plastic covers. How many plastic covers were needed to cover the court from the rain?

   Ⓐ 3 plastic covers
   Ⓑ 4 plastic covers
   Ⓒ 5 plastic covers
   Ⓓ 6 plastic covers

2. John eats a bowl of cereal for 3 of his 4 meals each day. He finishes two gallons of milk in eight days. How much milk does John use for one bowl of cereal? (Assume he only uses the milk for his cereal.)

   Ⓐ One-twelfth of a gallon of milk
   Ⓑ One cup of milk
   Ⓒ Two cups of milk
   Ⓓ One-sixth of a gallon of milk

3. A recipe to make a cake calls for three-fourths of a cup of milk. Mary used this cake as the first layer of a wedding cake. The second layer was half the size of the first layer, and the third layer was half the size of the second layer. How much milk would be used for the entire wedding cake?

   Ⓐ One and two-thirds cups of milk
   Ⓑ One and one-third cups of milk
   Ⓒ One and five-sixteenths cups of milk
   Ⓓ One cup of milk

4. One third of a quart of paint covers one fourth of a basketball court. How much paint does it take to paint the entire basketball court?

   Ⓐ one and one-third quarts
   Ⓑ one quart
   Ⓒ one and one-fourth quarts
   Ⓓ one and three-fourths quarts

5. **The total cost of 100 pencils purchased at a constant rate is $39.00. What is the unit price?**

   Ⓐ $39.00
   Ⓑ $3.90
   Ⓒ $0.39
   Ⓓ $0.039

6. **A construction worker was covering the bathroom wall with tiles. He covered three-fifths of the wall with 50 tiles. How many tiles will it take to cover the entire wall?**

   Ⓐ 83 tiles
   Ⓑ 83 and one-third tiles
   Ⓒ 85 tiles
   Ⓓ 83 and one-half tiles

7. **Jim ran four-fifths of a mile and dropped out of the 1600 meter race. His pace was 12 miles an hour until the point he dropped out of the race. How many minutes did he run?**

   Ⓐ 4 minutes and 30 seconds
   Ⓑ 4 minutes
   Ⓒ 4 minutes and 20 seconds
   Ⓓ 4 minutes and 10 seconds

8. **Ping played three-fourths of a football game. The game was three and a half hours long. How many hours did Ping play in this game?**

   Ⓐ 2 hours 37 minutes
   Ⓑ 2 hours 37 minutes and 30 seconds
   Ⓒ 2 hours 37 minutes and 20 seconds
   Ⓓ 2 hours 37 minutes and 10 seconds

9. **Bill is working out by running up and down the steps at the local stadium. He runs different number of steps in random order.**

   Which of the following is his best time of steps per minute?

   Ⓐ 25 steps in 5 minutes
   Ⓑ 30 steps in 5.5 minutes
   Ⓒ 20 steps in 4.5 minutes
   Ⓓ 15 steps in 4 minutes

10. Doogle drove thirty and one-third miles toward his brother's house in one-third of an hour. About how long will the entire hundred mile trip take at this constant speed?

Ⓐ 1 hour
Ⓑ 1 hour and 6 minutes
Ⓒ 1 hour and 1 minutes
Ⓓ 1 hour and 3 minutes

Chapter 3

Lesson 5: Finding Constant of Proportionality

1. **According to the graph, what is the constant of proportionality?**

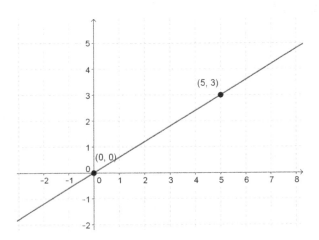

(5, 3)

(0, 0)

Ⓐ $\dfrac{3}{5}$

Ⓑ 5

Ⓒ 3

Ⓓ $\dfrac{1}{3}$

2. **According to the table, how much does one ticket cost?**

Number of Tickets	Total Cost
3	$ 21.00
4	$ 28.00
5	$ 35.00
6	$ 42.00

Ⓐ $21.00
Ⓑ $4.75
Ⓒ $7.00
Ⓓ $16.50

3. If y = 3x, what is the constant of proportionality between y and x?

   Ⓐ 1
   Ⓑ 0.30
   Ⓒ 1.50
   Ⓓ 3

4. When Frank buys three packs of pens, he knows he has 36 pens. When he buys five packs, he knows he has 60 pens. What is the constant of proportionality between the number of packs and the number of pens?

   Ⓐ 12
   Ⓑ 10
   Ⓒ 36
   Ⓓ 60

5. What is the unit rate for the number of hours of study each week per class?

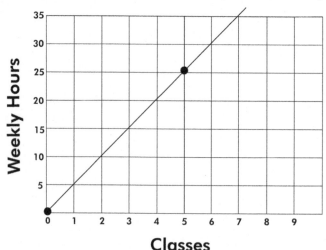

   Ⓐ 25 hours
   Ⓑ 5 hours
   Ⓒ 7 hours
   Ⓓ 10 hours

6. What is the constant of proportionality in the following equation?

   B = 1.25C

   Ⓐ 1.00
   Ⓑ 0.25
   Ⓒ 1.25
   Ⓓ 2.50

7. When Georgia buys 3 boxes of peaches, she has 40 pounds more than when she buys 1 box of peaches. How many pounds of peaches are in each box?

Ⓐ 40
Ⓑ 60
Ⓒ 20
Ⓓ 3

8. Look at the table below:

X	5	6	7	8
Y	90	108	126	144

What is the constant of proportionality of y to x. Enter your answer in the box given below.

9. Suppose the relationship between x and y is proportional. If the constant of proportionality of y to x is 16, select possible values for y and x.

Ⓐ x = 6 and y = 96
Ⓑ x = 96 and y = 6
Ⓒ x = 9 and y = 90
Ⓓ x = 144 and y = 9

Chapter 3

Lesson 6: Applying Ratios and Percents

1. **What value of x will make these two expressions equivalent?**

   $\dfrac{-3}{7}$ and $\dfrac{x}{21}$

   Ⓐ x = -3
   Ⓑ x = 7
   Ⓒ x = 9
   Ⓓ x = -9

2. **If p varies proportionally to s, and p = 10 when s = 2, which of the following equations correctly models this relationship?**

   Ⓐ p = 5s
   Ⓑ p = 10s
   Ⓒ s = 10p
   Ⓓ 2s = 10p

3. **Solve for x, if** $\dfrac{72}{108}$ **and** $\dfrac{x}{54}$ **are equivalent.**

   Ⓐ x = 18
   Ⓑ x = 36
   Ⓒ x = 54
   Ⓓ x = 24

4. **At one particular store, the sale price, s, is always 75% of the displayed price, d. Which of the following equations correctly shows how to calculate s from d?**

   Ⓐ d = 75s
   Ⓑ s = 0.75d
   Ⓒ s = d - 0.75
   Ⓓ s = d + 75

5. When x = 6, y = 4. If y is proportional to x, what is the value for y when x = 9?

    Ⓐ 4
    Ⓑ $\dfrac{2}{3}$
    Ⓒ 3
    Ⓓ 6

6. Jim is shopping for a suit to wear to his friend's wedding. He finds the perfect one on sale at 30% off. If the original price was $250.00, what will the selling price be after the discount?

    Ⓐ $75
    Ⓑ $175
    Ⓒ $200
    Ⓓ $220

7. If Julie bought her prom dress on sale at 15% off and paid $110.49 before tax, find the original price of her dress.

    Ⓐ $126.55
    Ⓑ $129.99
    Ⓒ $135.00
    Ⓓ $139.99

8. A plot of land is listed for sale with the following measurements: 1300 ft x 982 ft. When the buyer measured the land, he found that it measured 1285 ft by 982 ft. What was the % of error of the area of the plot?

    Ⓐ 1.47%
    Ⓑ 14.73%
    Ⓒ 1.15%
    Ⓓ 11.7%

9. Pierre received a parking ticket whose cost is $22.00. Each month that he failed to make payment, fees of $7.00 were added. By the time he paid the ticket, his bill was $36.00. What was the ratio of fees to the cost of the ticket?

Ⓐ $\dfrac{36}{22}$

Ⓑ $\dfrac{22}{36}$

Ⓒ $\dfrac{7}{22}$

Ⓓ $\dfrac{7}{11}$

10. Sara owns a used furniture store. She bought a chest for $42 and sold it for $73.50. What percent did she mark up the chest?

Ⓐ 100%
Ⓑ 75%
Ⓒ 42%
Ⓓ 31.5%

Chapter 3

Lesson 7: Modeling Using Equations or Inequalities

1. A 30 gallon overhead tank was slowly filled with water through a tap. The amount of water (W, in gallons) that is filled over a period of t hours can be found using W = 3.75(t). If the tap is opened at 7 AM and closed at 3 PM, how much water would be in the tank? Assume that the tank is empty before opening the tap.

   Ⓐ 18 gallons
   Ⓑ 20 gallons
   Ⓒ 24 gallons
   Ⓓ The tank is full

2. The ratio (by volume) of milk to water in a certain solution is 3 to 8. If the total volume of the solution is 187 cubic feet, what is the volume of water in the solution?

   Ⓐ 130 cubic feet
   Ⓑ 132 cubic feet
   Ⓒ 134 cubic feet
   Ⓓ 136 cubic feet

3. A box has a length of 12 inches and width of 10 inches. If the volume of the box is 960 cubic inches, what is its height?

   Ⓐ 6 inches
   Ⓑ 10 inches
   Ⓒ 12 inches
   Ⓓ 8 inches

4. Jan is planting tomato plants in her garden. Last year she planted 24 plants and harvested 12 bushels of tomatoes during the season. This year she has decided to only plant 18 plants. If the number of plants is directly proportional to the number of bushels of tomatoes harvested, how many bushels of tomatoes should she expect this year?

   Ⓐ 6
   Ⓑ 18
   Ⓒ 12
   Ⓓ 9

5. Melanie's age added to Roni's age is 27. Roni's age subtracted from Melanie's age is 3. Find their ages.

    Ⓐ 17, 10
    Ⓑ 16, 11
    Ⓒ 15, 12
    Ⓓ 14, 13

6. Which of the following expressions represents "5% of a number"?

    Ⓐ 5n
    Ⓑ 0.5n
    Ⓒ 0.05n
    Ⓓ 500n

7. Jill is shopping at a department store that is having a sale this week. The store has advertised 15% off certain off-season merchandise. Jill calculates the sales price by multiplying the regular price by 15% and then subtracting that amount from the regular price: SP = RP - 0.15(RP), where SP = Sales Price and RP = Regular Price. Find a simpler way for Jill to calculate the sales price as she shops.

    Ⓐ SP = 0.15 RP
    Ⓑ SP = 1.15 RP
    Ⓒ SP = 0.85 RP
    Ⓓ SP = 1.85 RP

8. Rewrite the following expression for the perimeter of a rectangle.

    P = l + w + l + w, where P = perimeter, l = length, and w = width.

    Ⓐ P = l + 2w
    Ⓑ P = l + w
    Ⓒ P = 2(l) + w
    Ⓓ P = 2(l + w)

9. To find the average of five consecutive integers beginning with x, we add the integers and divide by 5.

    Expressed in mathematical symbols, we have (x + x + 1+ x + 2 + x + 3 + x + 4) / 5 = Average (a)

    Rewrite this expression another way.

    Ⓐ x + 4
    Ⓑ x + 3
    Ⓒ x + 2
    Ⓓ None of the above.

10. If an item costs a store x dollars to buy and can be sold at y dollars, what percentage of the sale price is profit?

percentage of the sale price = [profit ÷ sale price] 100

Which of the following rewrites this expression and includes the given information?

Ⓐ $\dfrac{y - x}{100y}$

Ⓑ $\dfrac{100(y - x)}{y}$

Ⓒ $\dfrac{x - y}{100y}$

Ⓓ $\dfrac{100(x - y)}{y}$

Chapter 3

Lesson 8: Linear Inequality Word Problems

1. The annual salary for a certain position depends upon the years of experience of the applicant. The base salary is $50,000, and an additional $3,000 is added to that per year of experience, y, in the field. The company does not want to pay more than $70,000 for this position, though. Which of the following inequalities correctly expresses this scenario?

   (A) $53,000y \leq 70,000$
   (B) $3,000y \leq 50,000$
   (C) $50,000 + 3,000y \leq 70,000$
   (D) $3,000 + 50,000y \leq 70,000$

2. Huck has $225 in savings, and he is able to save an additional $45 per week from his work income. He wants to save enough money to have at least $500 in his savings. If w is the number of weeks, express this situation as an inequality.

   (A) $265w \geq 500$
   (B) $225 + 45w \geq 500$
   (C) $225 \leq 45w$
   (D) $225 + 45w \leq 500$

3. Lucy is charging her phone. It has a 20% charge right now and increases by an additional 2% charge every 3 minutes. She doesn't want to take it off the charger until it is at least 75% charged. If m is the number of minutes Lucy keeps her phone for charging, express this situation in an inequality.

   (A) $20 + \dfrac{2}{3}\, m \leq 75$

   (B) $20m + \dfrac{2}{3}\, m \leq 75$

   (C) $75 + \dfrac{2}{3}\, m \geq 20$

   (D) $20 + \dfrac{2}{3}\, m \geq 75$

4. Matt's final grade, G, in class depends on his last test score, t, according to the expression $G = 74 + 0.20t$. If he wants to have a final grade of at least 90.0, what is the minimum score he can make on the test?

Ⓐ 80
Ⓑ 74
Ⓒ 92
Ⓓ 86

5. Students can figure out their grade, G, on the test based upon how many questions they miss, n. The formula for their grade is $G = 100 - 4n$. If Tim wants to make at least an 83, what is the maximum number of questions he can miss?

Ⓐ 5 questions
Ⓑ 3 questions
Ⓒ 4 questions
Ⓓ 6 questions

6. The necessary thickness, T, of a steel panel in mm depends on the unsupported length, L, of the panel in feet according to the inequality $T \geq 3 + 0.2L$. If the thickest panel available has a thickness of 12 mm, what is the maximum length it can span?

Ⓐ 75 ft
Ⓑ 45 ft
Ⓒ 60 ft
Ⓓ 54 ft

7. The pay that a salesperson receives each week is represented by the inequality $P \geq 300 + 25s$, where s represents the number of units the salesperson sells. What is the significance of the number 300 in this inequality in this context?

Ⓐ The salesperson will never make more than $300 weekly.
Ⓑ The salesperson has never sold more than 300 units in a week.
Ⓒ The salesperson is guaranteed at least $300 even if he doesn't sell any units.
Ⓓ $300 is the price of a single unit.

8. The net calories gained or lost by a dieter depends on the hours exercised in a week according to the equation $C = 750 - 200h$. Based on his goals, Neil determines that the following inequality is necessary for him: $h > 3.75$. What is the significance of the value of this inequality?

Ⓐ Neil will lose at least 3.75 pounds per week if he meets this inequality.
Ⓑ Neil will lose weight each week if he meets this inequality.
Ⓒ Neil can eat only 375 calories on any given day.
Ⓓ If Neil meets this inequality, he will be able to eat as many calories as he likes.

9. **A school always allows twice as many girls as boys to enroll in swimming classes each year. They also follow a certain inequality for the number of boys, B, and girls, G, in their admissions: B + G ≤ 300. What significance does this inequality have for the number of boys that can be admitted each year?**

Ⓐ At least 200 boys must be admitted.
Ⓑ No more than 100 boys can be admitted.
Ⓒ The number of boys admitted must equal the number of girls.
Ⓓ No more than 150 boys can be admitted.

10. **Isaac has to do at least 4 hours of chores each week. For each hour of television he watches, that minimum number of hours increases by 0.25. This week, the inequality for his hours of chores is h ≥ 5.5. What does this indicate about his television watching?**

Circle the correct answer choice.

Ⓐ He watched 6 hours of television this week.
Ⓑ He watched 5.5 hours of television this week.
Ⓒ He watched 22 hours of television this week.
Ⓓ He watched no television this week.

Chapter 3

Lesson 9: Real world problem using inequality

1. Bob, the plumber, charges $\frac{1}{4}$ the cost of materials as his labor fee. If his current job has a material cost of $130, how much will Bob charge his client (including his labor fee)?

   Ⓐ $162.50
   Ⓑ $32.50
   Ⓒ $130.25
   Ⓓ None of the above

2. A box has a length of 6x inches. The width equals one third the length, and the height equals half the length. If the volume equals 972 cubic inches, what does x equal?

   Ⓐ 5
   Ⓑ 2
   Ⓒ 3
   Ⓓ 4

3. Taylor is trimming the shrubbery along three sides of his backyard. The backyard is rectangular in shape. The length of the backyard is twice its width and the total perimeter is 180 feet.

   The shrubbery that Taylor needs to trim is along three sides of the rectangular backyard (along the two lengths and one width). Find the total length of the shrubbery that he needs to trim.

   Ⓐ 180 ft
   Ⓑ 120 ft
   Ⓒ 90 ft
   Ⓓ 150 ft

4. Jim is 4 years older than his brother Bob. In two years, Jim will be twice Bob's age. How old are they now?

   Ⓐ Bob is 6 and Jim is 10.
   Ⓑ Bob is 4 and Jim is 8.
   Ⓒ Bob is 0 and Jim is 4.
   Ⓓ Bob is 2 and Jim is 6.

5. In a certain classroom, the ratio of boys to girls is 2 to 1. If there are 39 students in the classroom, how many are boys?

Ⓐ 18
Ⓑ 22
Ⓒ 26
Ⓓ 30

6 The bank will charge a 10% overdraft fee for any money withdrawn over the amount available in an account. If Jared has d dollars in the bank and he withdraws (d + 5) dollars, the bank charges 0.10{(d + 5) - d}. Find a simpler way of rewriting his overdraft fee.

Ⓐ 0.10(d + 5)
Ⓑ $0.50
Ⓒ $5.00
Ⓓ $2.50

7. Bob has been logging the days that the temperature rises over 100° in Orlando. He found that on 18 of the past 30 days the temperature rose above 100°.

Using this information, he made the following prediction of the number of days out of the next n days that the temperature would NOT rise above 100°:

$P = \left| \dfrac{30 - 18}{30} \right|$ n days. Find another way to write this expression.

Ⓐ $\left(\dfrac{2}{5}\right)$ n days

Ⓑ $\left(\dfrac{3}{5}\right)$ n days

Ⓒ $\left(\dfrac{4}{5}\right)$ n days

Ⓓ n days

8. If Roni runs for 20 minutes, walks for 10 and then runs for 15 while covering a total distance of m miles, her rate would be represented by:

r = m /{(20 + 10 +15) / 60} mph. Which of the following is a simpler representation of this formula?

Ⓐ r =(m/45) mph
Ⓑ r = (4/3m) mph
Ⓒ r = (45m/60) mph
Ⓓ r = (4m/3) mph

9. The diameter of the Sun at the equator is 1,400,000 km. d = 1,400,000 km

   Which of the following is another way to write this expression?

   Ⓐ $d = 1.4 \times 10^6$ km
   Ⓑ $d = 1.4 \times 10^{-6}$ km
   Ⓒ $d = 14 \times 10^6$ km
   Ⓓ $d = 14 \times 10^{-6}$ km

10. Which is another way of writing the following mathematical expression?

    (6x - 15y - 2x + y) / -4(x - y)

    Ⓐ $\dfrac{2x - 7y}{-2x - 2y}$

    Ⓑ $\dfrac{2x - 7y}{-2}$

    Ⓒ 5/2

    Ⓓ $\dfrac{2x - 7y}{-2(x-y)}$

Chapter 3

Lesson 10: Equations and Inequalities

1. How many positive whole number solutions (values for x) does this inequality have?
   x ≤ 20

   Ⓐ 19
   Ⓑ 20
   Ⓒ 21
   Ⓓ Infinite

2. Which of the following correctly shows the number sentence that the following words describe? 17 is less than or equal to the product of 6 and q.

   Ⓐ $17 \le 6q$
   Ⓑ $17 \le 6 - q$
   Ⓒ $17 < 6q$
   Ⓓ $17 \ge 6q$

3. Which of the following correctly shows the number sentence that the following words describe? The quotient of d and 5 is 15.

   Ⓐ $\dfrac{5}{d} = 15$

   Ⓑ $5d = 15$

   Ⓒ $\dfrac{d}{5} = 15$

   Ⓓ $d - 5 = 15$

4. Which of the following correctly shows the number sentence that the following words describe? Three times the quantity u – 4 is less than 17

   Ⓐ $3(u - 4) > 17$
   Ⓑ $3(u - 4) < 17$
   Ⓒ $3(u - 4) \le 17$
   Ⓓ $3(u - 4) \ge 17$

5. Which of the following correctly shows the number sentence that the following words describe? The difference between z and the quantity 7 minus r is 54.

Ⓐ $z - 7 - r = 54$
Ⓑ $z + 7 - r = 54$
Ⓒ $z + (7 - r) = 54$
Ⓓ $z - (7 - r) = 54$

6. Which of the following correctly shows the number sentence that the following words describe? The square of the sum of 6 and b is greater than 10.

Ⓐ $(6 + b)^2 > 10$
Ⓑ $6^2 + b^2 > 10$
Ⓒ $(6 + b)^2 = 10$
Ⓓ $(6 + b)^2 < 10$

7. Which of the following correctly shows the number sentence that the following words describe? 16 less than the product of 5 and h is 21.

Ⓐ $16 - 5h = 21$
Ⓑ $5h - 16 = 21$
Ⓒ $16 - (5 + h) = 21$
Ⓓ $16 < 5h + 21$

8. Which of the following correctly shows the number sentence that the following words describe? 8 times the quantity 2x – 7 is greater than 5 times the quantity 3x + 9.

Ⓐ $8(2x) - 7 > 5(3x) + 9$
Ⓑ $8(2x - 7) \geq 5(3x + 9)$
Ⓒ $8(2x - 7) > 5(3x + 9)$
Ⓓ $8(2x - 7) < 5(3x + 9)$

9. A batting cage offers 8 pitches for a quarter. Raul has $1.50. Which expression could be used to calculate how many pitches Raul could get for his money?

Ⓐ $\$1.50 \times 8$
Ⓑ $\$1.50 \div 8$
Ⓒ $(\$1.50 \div \$0.25) \times 8$
Ⓓ $(\$1.50 \div \$0.25)$

10. For which of the following values of x is this inequality true?
    $500 - 3x > 80$

    (A) $x = 140$
    (B) $x = 150$
    (C) $x = 210$
    (D) $x = 120$

End of Computations and Algebraic Relationships

Answer Key and Detailed Explanations

Chapter 3:
Computations and Algebraic Relationships

Lesson 1: Rational Numbers, Multiplication & Division

Question No.	Answer	Detailed Explanations
1	C	Divide 7 by 8 using long division, and the result is 0.875.
2	A	Divide 5 by 6 using long division. The decimal repeats endlessly: 0.83333...
3	A	If the decimal terminates, then the number can always be written as the quotient of two integers and is rational.
4	A	Divide 4 by 11 using long division. The decimal repeats endlessly: 0.363636...
5	B	If the decimal repeats endlessly, the number can be expressed as a quotient of integers and is rational.
6	A	Remember that when we multiply like signs, either (- * -) or (+ * +), the result is positive, and when we multiply unlike signs, the result is negative. Since we are multiplying some number by - 9 and get +36, we know that the sign of the unknown quantity is also negative. Now, 4 * 9 = 36; so - 4 * - 9 = 36. - 4 is the correct answer.
7	C	x = (-2)(6)(-4) = 48. Option C is the correct answer.
8	B	To arrive at the answer, multiply 53 by 116 (without considering decimal places). The answer got is 6148. there are 2 digits after decimal place in multiplicand (0.53) and 1 digit after decimal place in the multiplier (11.6). Hence, we need to place the decimal point after the 3rd digit (2+1) when counting from right. So, the answer will be 6.148
9	C	Rational numbers are numbers that can be written as p/q where p & q are integers and q is not 0. To remember this definition, associate rational with ratio. √3 is the correct answer.
10	A	If the sum of the digits is divisible by 3, then the number is divisible by 3. The sum of the digits of 459,732 is 30 which is divisible by 3. Therefore, 459,732 is divisible by 3. 459,732 is the correct answer.

Lesson 2: Apply and extend previous understandings of operations

Question No.	Answer	Detailed Explanations
1	B	$15.00 - $9.39 = $ 5.61 is the correct answer.
2	B	50.75 x 25 = 1268.75 pounds 1268.75 pounds. Option B is the correct answer.
3	A	1528.80 pounds ÷ 50 bags = 30.576 pounds in each bag. Option A is the correct answer.
4	C	To solve this problem, list all the monetary values, along with the proper operation, before evaluating it. For this problem, words like "give" mean to subtract, while "receives" means to add. (1) 76.00 - 42.45 - 21.34 + 14.50 = (2) 33.55 - 21.34 + 14.50 = (3) 12.21 + 14.50 = (4) 26.71 Therefore, John will have $26.71 later that night.
5	B	Remember: adding and subtracting rational numbers works just like integers. If you need to carry or borrow, the rules remain the same. 25 + 2.005 - 7.253 - 2.977 27.005 - 7.253 - 2.977 , 19.752 - 2.977 = 16.775
6	D	The pizza was divided equally so each person's cost for pizza is $17.49 ÷ 5 = $3.50. Soda was $1.19 each. Add to find the total cost for each person. $3.50 + $1.19 = $4.69. $4.69 is the correct answer.
7	D	On his second trip to the store he paid $74.99 plus half of $68.55. $74.99 + $34.28 = $109.27 $159.95 - 109.27 = $50.68 $50.68 is the correct answer.
8	B	First, we will change 5 1/2 to 5.5. Then we have 3.24 - 1.914 - 6.025 +9.86 -2.2 + 5.5 = 8.461 8.461 is the correct answer.

Question No.	Answer	Detailed Explanations
9	A	2 bagels @ $0.69 each = 2 x $0.69 = $1.38 3 yogurts @ $1.49 each = 3 x $1.49 = $4.47 1 orange juice @ $1.75 = $1.75 Total bill = $7.60 $7.60 is the correct answer.
10	A	Year 1 - $12.00, Year 2 - $24.00. Year 3 - $36.00. Year 4 - $48.00. Year 5 - $60.00. Year 6 - $72.00. Year 7 - $84.00. Year 8 - $96.00. Year 9 - $108.00. Year 10 - $120.00 Adding the totals for each year, we get $660.00. $660.00 is the correct answer.

Lesson 3: Represent proportions by equations

Question No.	Answer	Detailed Explanations
1	B	Divide the total cost by the number of hats: $\frac{18}{3} = 6$. This gives the cost per hat, which is the constant of proportionality in the equation: $C = 6n$.
2	A	Choose a pair of data. Divide the value of y by the value of x: $\frac{14}{1} = 14$. This gives the constant of proportionality in the equation: $y = 14x$.
3	D	Divide the total cost by the number of months: $\frac{100}{4} = 25$. This gives the cost per month, which is the constant of proportionality in the equation: $C = 25m$.
4	C	Divide the total cost by the number of pounds: $\frac{4.50}{5} = 0.9$. This gives the cost per pound, which is the constant of proportionality in the equation: $C = 0.9p$.
5	A	Divide the rental cost by the area of the apartment: $\frac{600}{800} = 0.75$. This gives the cost per square foot of area, which is the constant of proportionality in the equation: $C = 0.75a$.
6	B	Divide the total cost by the number of desks: $\frac{7000}{350} = 20$. This gives the cost per desk, which is the constant of proportionality in the equation: $C = 20d$.
7	A	Divide the total number of players by the number of teams: $\frac{180}{12} = 15$. This gives the number of players per team, which is the constant of proportionality in the equation: $p = 15t$.
8	D	The relationship named is that between cost and the number of packs. The number of rolls per pack is irrelevant. The cost per pack is already given as $5 per pack, so this is the constant of proportionality in the equation: $C = 5p$
9	B	Divide the total cost by the number of loads: $\frac{1750}{5} = 350$. This gives the cost per load, which is the constant of proportionality in the equation: $C = 350g$.
10	A	The straight line passes through the origin, so the relationship is proportional. Use the values of a point on the line. Divide the pay by the number of hours: $\frac{50}{4} = 12.50$. This gives the pay per hour, which is the constant of proportionality in the equation: $P = 12.50h$.

Lesson 4: Unit Rates

Question No.	Answer	Detailed Explanations
1	B	First, find out the area of the tennis court. (1) $25 \times 20 = 500$ square feet Next, find out the area of one plastic cover (2) $13 \times 10 = 130$ square feet Divide 500 by 130 (3) $500 \div 130 = 3.84$ Therefore, 4 plastic covers are needed for the tennis court.
2	A	First, find out how much cereal John eats in 8 days: (1) 3 bowls per day x 8 days = 24 bowls. Since it takes 2 gallons of milk to eat 24 bowls of cereal, set up the ratio and simplify: (2) $\frac{2}{24}$ (GCF is 2, so divide numerator and denominator to find simplest form) (3) $\frac{1}{12}$ Therefore, John uses $\frac{1}{12}$ of a gallon of milk in each bowl of cereal.
3	C	To solve this problem, first, find the amount of milk required for each layer. For the first layer, $\frac{3}{4}$ cup of milk is required. Since the second layer is half the size, the amount of milk required will be $\frac{3}{4} \times \frac{1}{2} = \frac{3}{8}$ cups are required. For the third layer, which is half of layer two, the milk required will be $\frac{3}{8} \times \frac{1}{2} = \frac{3}{16}$ of a cup. The total milk required will be $\frac{3}{4} + \frac{3}{8} + \frac{3}{16}$ To add, find the LCD, which is 16 in this case. Hence, $\frac{3}{4} + \frac{3}{8} + \frac{3}{16}$ represented by LCD will become $(\frac{3}{4} \times \frac{4}{4}) + (\frac{3}{8} \times \frac{2}{2}) + \frac{3}{16}$ $= \frac{12}{16} + \frac{6}{16} + \frac{3}{16} = \frac{21}{16}$ Converting this to mixed fraction we get, $1\frac{5}{16}$. Hence, the correct answer choice is Option C.

Question No.	Answer	Detailed Explanations
4	A	If $\frac{1}{4}$ th of a basketball court can be covered by $\frac{1}{3}$ rd of a quart of paint then to cover the entire court 4 times the amount required for covering $\frac{1}{4}$ th of a court would be required. Therefore, Paint required to cover the entire court $= \frac{1}{3} \times 4 = \frac{4}{3} = 1\frac{1}{3}$
5	C	Unit price means price per one unit. Therefore, we need to know the price per pencil. Since the price of the pencils is defined to be a constant rate, then the total cost ($39.00) divided by the total number of pencils (100) will give us the cost per pencil (or per unit). $39.00 / 100 = $0.39 per pencil The unit price is $0.39. The correct answer is $0.39.
6	B	To solve this problem, find out how much it takes to cover 1/5 of the wall, and then multiply by 5. (1) $50 \div 3 =$ (how much it takes to cover 1/5 of the bathroom wall) (2) multiply $16.66 \times 5 = 83.33$ (3) $83.33 = 83\frac{1}{3}$ Therefore, it will take 83 and one-third tiles to cover the entire wall.
7	B	To solve this problem, set up a proportion: (distance)/(time) = (distance)/(time) Plug in the numbers (you can convert to decimals to simplify the process): $\frac{0.8 \text{ mile}}{x \text{ min}} = \frac{12 \text{ miles}}{60 \text{ min}}$. Using cross products $a/b = c/d$ is $ad = bc$ $(0.8)(60) = (x)(12)$ $48 = 12x$ (solve for x by dividing each side by 12) $4 = x$. Therefore, Jim ran 4 minutes.
8	B	To solve this problem, multiply $\frac{3}{4} \times 3\frac{1}{2}$ (1). Convert $3\frac{1}{2}$ to an improper fraction $= \frac{7}{2}$ (2) $\frac{3}{4} \times \frac{7}{2} =$ (3) $\frac{3 \times 7}{4 \times 2} =$ (4) $\frac{21}{8}$ (convert back to a mixed number)(5) $2\frac{5}{8}$ (6) $\frac{5}{8} = 37.5$ minutes. Therefore, Ping played 2 hours 37 minutes and 30 seconds.

Question No.	Answer	Detailed Explanations
9	B	To answer the question we must find in which case he ran the most steps per minute. Since he is running up and down, we double the number of steps; so $\dfrac{50}{5}$ = 10 steps per minute $\dfrac{60}{5.5}$ = 10.9 steps per minute * (when rounded to the nearest tenth) $\dfrac{40}{4.5}$ = 8.9 steps per minute (when rounded to the nearest tenth) $\dfrac{30}{4}$ = 7.5 steps per minute 30 steps in 5.5 minutes gives an average of 10.9 steps per minute which is his best time. 30 steps in 5.5 minutes is the correct answer. (Note : If we don't double the steps, then also answer does not change. Only the number of steps per minute will differ)
10	B	To solve this problem, set up a proportion: (distance)/(time) = (distance)/(time) $\dfrac{1}{3}$ of an hour is equivalent to 20 minutes. Plug in the numbers (you can convert to decimals to simplify the process): $\dfrac{30.33 \text{ miles}}{20 \text{ minutes}} = \dfrac{100 \text{ miles}}{x \text{ minutes}}$. Using cross products a/b = c/d is ad = bc (30.33)(x) = (20)(100) 30.33x = 2000 (solve for x by dividing each side by 30.33) x = 65.94 (round up to the nearest whole number). Since 65.94 is almost 66 minutes, that is the same as one hour and 6 minutes.

Lesson 5: Finding Constant of Proportionality

Question No.	Answer	Detailed Explanations
1	A	The line passes through the origin, so it is a proportional relationship. The second point gives the constant of proportionality, which is the y value divided by the x value: $\frac{3}{5}$.
2	C	For any of the pairs of data, divide the total cost by the number of tickets to find how much one ticket costs. For example, $\frac{\$21}{3} = \$7$ per ticket.
3	D	Because the equation is solved for y and is equal to a multiple of x, the coefficient of the x term gives the constant of proportionality: 3.
4	A	Divide the number of pens by the number of packs for either pair of data. For example, $\frac{36}{3} = 12$ pens per pack.
5	B	The line passes through the origin, so it is a proportional relationship. The second point gives the constant of proportionality, which is the y value divided by the x value: $\frac{25}{5}$, which simplifies to 5.
6	C	Because the equation is solved for y and is equal to a multiple of x, the coefficient of the x term gives the constant of proportionality: 1.25.
7	C	The difference between our two pairs of data is 2 boxes and 40 pounds of peaches. Divide the difference in pounds by the difference in boxes: $\frac{40}{2} = 20$ pounds per box.
8	18	The constant of proportionality is 18 because the relationship between x and y is to multiply by 18. For example, 5x18=90, 6x18=108, 7x18=126, 8x18=144. You can find this by dividing y by x.
9	A	The constant of proportionality of y to x is determined by dividing y by x. Because $\frac{96}{6} = 16$.

Lesson 6: Applying Ratios and Percents

Question No.	Answer	Detailed Explanations
1	D	In a set of equivalent ratios, or a proportion, the numerator and denominator of one ratio will be multiplied by the same number to get the values of the other ratio. In this case, the denominator of the first ratio, 7, is multiplied by 3 to get to 21. This means (-3) must also be multiplied by 3 to get to (-9).
2	A	To find the constant of proportionality, find the relationship between p and s. When p = 10 and s = 2, dividing p by s shows that p is 5 times s. Therefore, the equation that shows the constant of proportionality is p = 5s.
3	B	To solve this proportion for x, multiply both sides of the equation by 54, and simplify the result, We get, x = 36.
4	B	To find the constant of proportionality, find the relationship between s and d. s is 75% of d, which is the same as 0.75 times d. Therefore, the equation that shows the constant of proportionality is s = 0.75d.
5	D	Set up a proportion between the known ratio and the unknown ratio, and solve for y. $\dfrac{6}{4} = \dfrac{9}{y}$ $6y = 9\,(4)$ Cross Multiply $6y = 36$ Simplify $\dfrac{6y}{6} = \dfrac{36}{6}$ Divide each side by 6 $y = 6$ Simplify
6	B	Selling price (sp) = Original price (op) - 0.30(op) sp = 250 - 0.30(250) sp = 250 - 75 sp = 175. $175 is the correct answer.
7	B	Original price (op) - 0.15(op) = Selling price (sp) op - 0.15(op) = 110.49 0.85(op) = 110.49 $op = \dfrac{110.49}{0.85}$ op = $129.99. $129.99 is the correct answer.

Question No.	Answer	Detailed Explanations
8	C	Using original measurements, Area=1300 x 982=1,276,600 sq ft. Using actual measurements, Area=1285 x 982=1,261,870 sq ft. Error = 14,730 sq ft. $\dfrac{14,730}{1,276,600} \times 100 = 1.15\%$ error. The correct answer is 1.15%. Alternate Explanation : Since width is same in both the cases, we can write error $=\dfrac{\text{(original length x width) - (measured length x width)}}{\text{(original length x width)}}$ $=\dfrac{(1300 \times 982) - (1285 \times 982)}{(1300 \times 982)} = 982$ $\dfrac{1300 - 1285}{1300 \times 982}$. Since 982 is common factor in both numerator and denominator, error $=\dfrac{1300 - 1285}{1300} = \dfrac{15}{1300} = 0.0115 = 1.15\%$
9	D	$36.00 - \$22.00 = \$14.00$ in fees. $\dfrac{\$14.00}{\$22.00} = \dfrac{14}{22} = \dfrac{7}{11}$ is the ratio of fees to the cost of the ticket. $\dfrac{7}{11}$ is the correct answer.
10	B	Selling price - cost = markup $73.50 - \$42.00 = \$31.50$ markup markup percentage = markup/ cost *100 $\dfrac{\$31.50}{\$42} = 0.75 = 75\%$ markup. The correct answer is 75%.

Lesson 7: Modeling Using Equations or Inequalities

Question No.	Answer	Detailed Explanations
1	D	The first step to solving this problem is to figure out the value of t, the number of hours. As you know, 7 am to 3 pm represents 5 hours to 12 pm, then another 3 hours to 3pm, for a total of 8 hours. This gives us W = 3.75(8) = 30, a full tank.
2	D	Let the volume of water = w and volume of milk = m. m/w = 3/8. Rearranging the above equation, $m = \frac{3w}{8}$, m + w = 187 cubic ft. Replacing the value of m by $\frac{3w}{8}$ in the above equation, $\frac{3w}{8} + w = 187$, $\frac{11w}{8} = 187$, $w = \frac{187*8}{11} = 136$ cubic ft.
3	D	Remember: The volume of a rectangular box is V = lwh. This lets us set up the following equation: 960 = 12(10)h, 960 = 120h, 8 = h This gives us a height of 8 inches, as indicated.
4	D	Let b = the number of bushels harvested $\frac{24}{12} = \frac{18}{b}$, 24b = 12(18), 24b = 216, b = 9 bushels is the correct answer.
5	C	Let m = Melanie's age ; Then 27-m = Roni's Age ; m - (27-m) = 3 ; m - 27 + m = 3 ; 2m - 27 = 3 ; 2m = 3 + 27 ; 2m = 30 ; m = $\frac{30}{2}$=15 years=Melanie's Age ; Roni's Age=27-m=27-15=12 yrs. Alternative Explanation: Among the options, guess in which case the difference in age is 3 years. It is clear that option (C) is the correct answer.
6	C	A percent is a ratio that compares a number to 100. Therefore, 5% is 5 out of 100. To convert a percent to a decimal, divide by 100: 5 ÷ 100 = 0.05. To find 5% of a number, multiply the number times the decimal form of 5%: 0.05n. 0.05n is the correct answer.
7	C	SP = RP - 0.15(RP), SP = RP(1 - 0.15), SP = RP(0.85), SP = 0.85 RP is the correct answer.
8	D	P = l + w + l + w Combine like terms. P = 2(l) + 2(w) Factor out 2. P = 2(l + w) is the correct answer.
9	C	(x + x + 1+ x + 2 + x + 3 + x + 4) / 5 = Average (a) (5x + 10) / 5 = x + 2. x + 2 is the correct answer.
10	B	Percentage of the sale price = [profit ÷ sale price],100 = [(y - x) ÷ y], 100 = 100(y - x)/y is the correct answer.

Lesson 8: Linear Inequality Word Problems

Question No.	Answer	Detailed Explanations
1	C	3000 must be multiplied by y, the years of experience. This amount must then be added to the base salary of $50,000. This sum must be less than or equal to $70,000.
2	B	The weekly increase of 45 is multiplied by the number of weeks. This amount is added to the initial savings of 225. This sum must be greater than or equal to 500.
3	D	The number of minutes of charging time must be multiplied by 2 and divided by 3 to find the percentage of the battery that is charged over that time. This is then added to the initial charge of 20 percent, and the sum must be at least 75.
4	A	Set up an inequality that $74+0.20t \geq 90$. Solving for t, we find that $t \geq 80$.
5	C	Set up an inequality that $100 - 4n \geq 83$. Solving for n, we find that $n \leq 4.25$. Because you can only miss whole numbers of problems, the most he can miss is 4.
6	B	In the inequality, let T be 12, and solve for L. $12 \geq 3 + 0.2L$ ($\geq$ is to be read as greater than or equal to and $\leq$ as less than or equal to). $9 \geq 0.2L$ or $L \leq 9/0.2$ or $L \leq 45$. Therefore Maximum unsupported length for a panel of thickness 12 mm is 45 ft.
7	C	If the number of units sold is 0, the 300 is still present as the minimum amount of the pay. The 25 is multiplied by 0 in the equation and thus negated, but the 300 remains.
8	B	$C=750 - 200h$. If $h = 3.75$, $C = 750 - (200 \times 3.75) = 750 - 750 = 0$ So, if Neil does 3.75 hours of exercise in a week, he will not gain weight. If he does exercise for more than 3.75 hours, he will lose weight.
9	B	Because there are twice as many girls as boys to be admitted, girls must make up $\frac{2}{3}$ of the admitted group. This leaves one third to be boys. One third of 300 is 100.
10	A	His minimum hours of chores increased by 1.5 hours. This must represent 6 hours of TV watching that week .

Lesson 9: Real world problem using inequality

Question No.	Answer	Detailed Explanations
1	A	In order to find out how much Bill should charge his client, divide 130 by 4, and then add the quotient to 130: (1) $130 \div 4 = 32.50$ (2) $130 + 32.50 = \$162.50$
2	C	First, write the expressions based on the language in the problem: length = $6x$ width = $(\frac{1}{3})(6x)$ height = $(\frac{1}{2})(6x)$ Next, solve for x based on the formula for volume, lwh. (1) $6x \times ((\frac{1}{3})(6x)) \times ((\frac{1}{2})(6x)) = 972$ (2) $6x \times 2x \times 3x = 972$ (3) $12x^2 \times 3x = 972$ (4) $36x^3 = 972$ (divide each side by 36) (5) $x^3 = 27$ (6) $x = 3$
3	D	Let x be the width of the rectangular backyard. Length = $2x$. Perimeter of the backyard = $x + 2x + x + 2x = 180$ ft. $6x = 180$ ft. $x = \frac{180}{6} = 30$ ft. = width of the backyard. Length of the backyard = $2x = 60$ ft. Total length of the shrubbery Taylor needs to trim = width+length+length = $x + 2x + 2x = 150$ ft.
4	D	Now : Bob's age = x, Jim's age = x + 4 In 2 years : Bob's age = x + 2, Jim's age = x + 4 + 2 = x + 6 It is given that, in 2 years, Jim's age is twice Bob's age. Therefore, we have, x + 6 = 2(x + 2) x + 6 = 2x + 4 2 = x = Bob 6 = x + 4 = Jim Bob is 2, and Jim is 6.
5	C	Let x = number of girls, 2x = number of boys, x + 2x = 39, 3x = 39, x = 13, girls 2x = 26 boys
6	B	$0.10 (\$ (d + 5) - \$ d) = 0.10 (d + 5 - d) = 0.10(5)$ $\$0.50$ is the correct answer.
7	A	$(\frac{30-18}{30}) n = (\frac{12}{30}) n = (\frac{2}{5}) n$ days is the correct answer.
8	D	$r = m /[(20 + 10 + 15) / 60]$ $r = m / (\frac{45}{60}) = m / (\frac{3}{4}) = \frac{4m}{3}$ mph
9	A	Scientific notation is a simpler way to compute with very large or very small numbers. Using scientific notation, 1,400,000 km = 1.4×10^6 km 1.4×10^6 km is the correct answer.
10	D	$(6x - 15y - 2x + y) / -4(x - y) = (4x - 14y) / -4(x - y) = 2(2x - 7y) / -4(x - y) = (2x - 7y) / - 2(x - y)$ is the correct answer.

Lesson 10: Equations and Inequalities

Question No.	Answer	Detailed Explanations
1	B	x can be any whole number from 1 to 20, inclusive of 20.
2	A	"17 is less than or equal to" means 17 ≤ "the product of 6 and q" means to multiply 6 and q, or 6q 17 ≤ 6q
3	C	"The quotient of d and 5" means to divide d by 5 "is 15" means "equals 15". $\frac{d}{5} = 15$
4	B	"Three times the quantity u − 4" means to multiply (u−4) by 3 → 3(u−4) "is less than 17" means < 17 3(u−4) < 17
5	D	"The difference between z and the quantity 7 minus r" means to find the difference between z and (7−r), so z − (7−r) "is 54" means equals 54 So, z − (7 − r) = 54
6	A	"The square of the sum of 6 and b" means to square all of (6 + b), or $(6 + b)^2$ "is greater than 10" means "> 10" $(6 + b)^2 > 10$
7	B	"16 less than" means to "subtract 16 from some term" "the product of 5 and h" means to multiply 5 and h or "5h" "is 21" means "equals 21" 5h − 16 = 21
8	C	"8 times the quantity 2x − 7" means to multiply 8 and 2x − 7, which needs to be in parentheses (as a quantity), so 8(2x − 7) "is greater than" means ">" 5 times the quantity 3x + 9" means 5 multiplied by 3x + 9, which needs to be in parentheses (as a quantity), so 5(3x+9) 8(2x − 7) > 5(3x + 9)
9	C	To find how many quarters (or the equivalent of how many quarters) Raul has, you could calculate $1.50 divided by $0.25. Then, that amount of quarters would be multiplied by 8, the number of pitches purchased with each quarter. The final expression would read: ($1.50 ÷ $0.25) x 8

Question No.	Answer	Detailed Explanations
10	D	Solve to find x: $500 - 3x > 80$ First, subtract 500 from both sides $-3x > -420$ Next, divide both sides by -3. (Don't forget to switch the inequality sign when dividing a negative in an inequality) $x < 140$ So, $x = 120$ would work as a solution. To check: $500 - 3(120) = 500 - 360 = 140$, which is greater than 80.

Chapter 4

Geometry and Measurement

Chapter 4

Lesson 1: Application of proportion and unit rates using measurement

1. **Owen is 69 inches tall. How tall is Owen in feet?**

    Ⓐ 5.2 feet
    Ⓑ 5.75 feet
    Ⓒ 5.9 feet
    Ⓓ 6 feet

2. **What is 7 gallons 3 quarts expressed as quarts?**

    Ⓐ 4.75 quarts
    Ⓑ 28 quarts
    Ⓒ 29.2 quarts
    Ⓓ 31 quarts

3. **How many centimeters in 3.7 kilometers?**

    Ⓐ 0.000037 cm
    Ⓑ 0.037 cm
    Ⓒ 3700 cm
    Ⓓ 370,000 cm

4. **136 ounces is how many pounds?**

    Ⓐ 6.8 pounds
    Ⓑ 8.5 pounds
    Ⓒ 1088 pounds
    Ⓓ 2,176 pounds

5. **How many ounces in 5 gallons?**

    Ⓐ 128 ounces
    Ⓑ 320 ounces
    Ⓒ 640 ounces
    Ⓓ 1280 ounces

6. Lisa, Susan, and Chris participated in a three-person relay team. Lisa ran 1284 meters, Susan ran 1635 meters and Chris ran 1473 meters. How long was the race in kilometers? Round your answer to the nearest tenth.

   Ⓐ 4.0 km
   Ⓑ 4.4 km
   Ⓒ 43.9 km
   Ⓓ 49.0 km

7. Quita recorded the amount of time it took her to complete her chores each week for a month; 1 hour 3 minutes, 1 hour 18 minutes, 55 minutes, and 68 minutes. How many hours did Quita spend doing chores during the month?

   Ⓐ 3.8 hours
   Ⓑ 4.24 hours
   Ⓒ 4.4 hours
   Ⓓ 5.7 hours

8. Lamar can run 3 miles in 18 minutes. At this rate, how much distance he can run in one hour?

   Ⓐ 0.9 mph
   Ⓑ 1.1 mph
   Ⓒ 10 mph
   Ⓓ 21 mph

9. A rectangular garden has a width of 67 inches and a length of 92 inches. What is the perimeter of the garden in feet?

   Ⓐ 13.25 feet
   Ⓑ 26.5 feet
   Ⓒ 31.8 feet
   Ⓓ 42.8 feet

10. Pat has a pen pal in England. When Pat asked how tall his pen pal was he replied, 1.27 meters. If 1 inch is 2.54 cm, how tall is Pat's pen pal in feet and inches?

   Ⓐ 3 feet 11 inches
   Ⓑ 4 feet 2 inches
   Ⓒ 4 feet 6 inches
   Ⓓ 5 feet exactly

Chapter 4

Lesson 2: Drawing Plane (2-D) Figures

1. **Which of the following lengths cannot be the lengths of the sides of a triangle?**

   Ⓐ 4, 6, 9
   Ⓑ 3, 4, 2
   Ⓒ 2, 2, 3
   Ⓓ 1, 1, 2

2. **Which of the following set of lengths cannot be the lengths of the sides of a triangle?**

   Ⓐ 12.5, 20, 30
   Ⓑ 10, 10, 12
   Ⓒ 4, 8.5, 14
   Ⓓ 3, 3, 3

3. **If the measure of two angles in a triangle are 60 and 100 degrees, what is the measure of the third angle?**

   Ⓐ 20 degrees
   Ⓑ 50 degrees
   Ⓒ 30 degrees
   Ⓓ 180 degrees

4. **Which of the following triangle classifications does not describe the angles in a triangle?**

   Ⓐ Right
   Ⓑ Acute
   Ⓒ Equiangular
   Ⓓ Scalene

5. Which of the angles has the least measure?

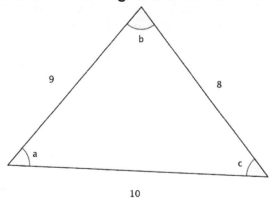

Ⓐ a
Ⓑ b
Ⓒ c
Ⓓ There is not enough information to tell

6. Find the value of x.

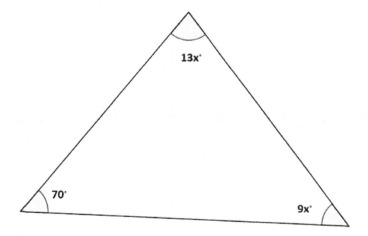

Ⓐ 6
Ⓑ 5
Ⓒ 10
Ⓓ 4

7. Which of the following lengths cannot be the lengths of the sides of a triangle?

Ⓐ 8, 12, 18
Ⓑ 6, 8, 4
Ⓒ 4, 4, 6
Ⓓ 2, 2, 4

8. If this is an isosceles triangle, which of the following could be the measure of each of the unknown angles? Take the sides which make up the angle 70° as equal to each other.

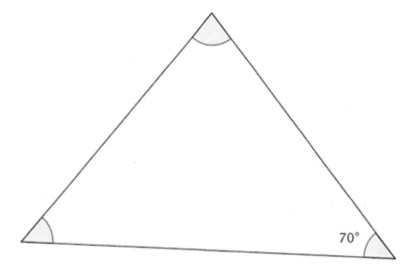

70°

Ⓐ 55°
Ⓑ 66°
Ⓒ 53°
Ⓓ 70°

9. Which of the following triangle classification is defined by an angle that is created by two perpendicular lines?

Ⓐ Right
Ⓑ Acute
Ⓒ Equiangular
Ⓓ Scalene

10. Which of the following triangle classifications is defined by three angles less than 90 degrees?

Ⓐ Right
Ⓑ Acute
Ⓒ Obtuse
Ⓓ Scalene

Chapter 4

Lesson 3: Circumference of a circle

1. A circle is divided into 4 equal sections. What is the measure of each of the angles formed at the center of the circle?

   Ⓐ 25°
   Ⓑ 180°
   Ⓒ 90°
   Ⓓ 360°

2. What is the area of a circle with diameter 8 cm? Round your answer to the nearest tenth. Use π = 3.14.

   Ⓐ 201.1 cm²
   Ⓑ 201.0 cm²
   Ⓒ 50.2 cm²
   Ⓓ 25.1 cm²

3. What is the radius of a circle with a circumference of 125 cm? Round your answer to the nearest whole number. Use π = 3.14.

   Ⓐ 24 cm
   Ⓑ 10 cm
   Ⓒ 20 cm
   Ⓓ **19 cm**

4. What is the circumference of a circle with radius 0.5 feet? Round your answer to the nearest tenth. Use π = 3.14.

   Ⓐ 3.1 ft
   Ⓑ 3.2 ft
   Ⓒ 0.8 ft
   Ⓓ 0.7 ft

5. Which of the following could constitute the area of a circle?

   Ⓐ 50 units
   Ⓑ 1 square unit
   Ⓒ 1.5 cubic units
   Ⓓ One half of a unit

6. If two radii form a 30 degree angle at the center of a circle with radius 10 cm, what is the area between them? Round your answer to the nearest tenth. Use π = 3.14.

    Hint: A circle "sweeps out" 360 degrees.

    Ⓐ 26.2 square centimeters
    Ⓑ 26.1 square centimeters
    Ⓒ 314.1 square centimeters
    Ⓓ 314.2 square centimeters

7. What is the area of a circle with radius 2.8 cm? Round your answer to the nearest tenth. Use π = 3.14.

    Ⓐ 24.7 cm²
    Ⓑ 24.6 cm²
    Ⓒ 17.6 cm²
    Ⓓ 8.8 cm²

8. What is the radius of a circle with area 50 square cm? Round your answer to the nearest whole number. Use π = 3.14.

    Ⓐ 4 cm
    Ⓑ 3 cm
    Ⓒ 8 cm
    Ⓓ 7 cm

9. What is the length of a semi-circle (curved part only) with radius 8 in? Round your answer to the nearest tenth. Use π = 3.14.

    Hint: A semi-circle is half a circle.

    Ⓐ 201.0 in
    Ⓑ 50.2 in
    Ⓒ 100.5 in
    Ⓓ 25.1 in

10. What is the diameter of a circle with an area of 50.24 m²? Use π = 3.14.

    Ⓐ 4 m
    Ⓑ 6 m
    Ⓒ 8 m
    Ⓓ 16 m

Chapter 4

Lesson 4: Solve mathematical and real-world problems

1. Triangle ABC and triangle PQR are similar. Find the value of x.

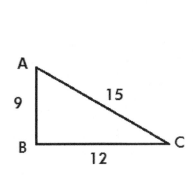 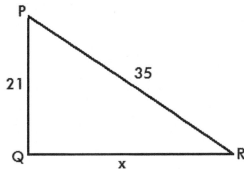

- Ⓐ 23
- Ⓑ 25
- Ⓒ 26
- Ⓓ 28

2. If the sides of two similar figures have a similarity ratio of $\dfrac{3}{2}$ what is the ratio of their areas?

- Ⓐ $\dfrac{9}{4}$

- Ⓑ $\dfrac{3}{2}$

- Ⓒ $\dfrac{1}{3}$

- Ⓓ $\dfrac{3}{1}$

3. **What is the similarity ratio between the following two similar figures?**

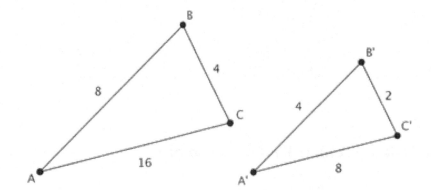

Ⓐ $\dfrac{2}{1}$

Ⓑ $\dfrac{1}{4}$

Ⓒ $\dfrac{2}{3}$

Ⓓ $\dfrac{3}{2}$

4. **A map is designed with a scale of 1 inch for every 5 miles. If the distance between two towns is 3 inches on the map, how far apart are they?**

Ⓐ 15 miles
Ⓑ 3 miles
Ⓒ 5 miles
Ⓓ 1.5 miles

5. **If the angles of one of two similar triangles are 30, 60, and 90 degrees, what are the angles for the other triangle?**

Ⓐ 60, 120, 180
Ⓑ 45, 45, 90
Ⓒ 30, 60, 90
Ⓓ There is not enough information to determine.

6. **The horizontal cross section of a square pyramid is a _____.**

   Ⓐ Square
   Ⓑ Circle
   Ⓒ Trapezoid
   Ⓓ Triangle

7. **In order for a three-dimensional shape to be classified as a "prism," its horizontal cross-sections must be _____.**

   Ⓐ congruent polygons
   Ⓑ non-congruent polygons
   Ⓒ circles
   Ⓓ equilateral triangles

8. **Which of the following nets is NOT the net of a cube?**

   Ⓐ

   Ⓑ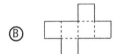

   Ⓒ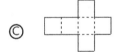

   Ⓓ

9. **The horizonal cross section of a pentagonal prism is a _____.**

   Ⓐ Triangle
   Ⓑ Pentagon
   Ⓒ Trapezoid
   Ⓓ Square

10. The vertical cross section of a cube is a _____.

- Ⓐ Square
- Ⓑ Triangle
- Ⓒ Circle
- Ⓓ Trapezoid

Chapter 4

Lesson 5: Finding Area, Volume, & Surface Area

1. **Find the area of the rectangle shown below.**

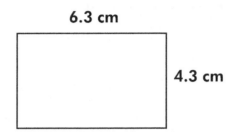

6.3 cm

4.3 cm

Ⓐ 10.5 square centimeters
Ⓑ 24 square centimeters
Ⓒ 27.09 square centimeters
Ⓓ 21 square centimeters

2. **What is the volume of a cube whose sides measure 8 inches?**

Ⓐ 24 in³
Ⓑ 64 in³
Ⓒ 128 in³
Ⓓ 512 in³

3. **Calculate the area of the following polygon.**

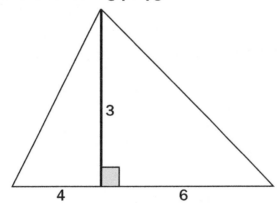

3

4   6

Ⓐ 15 square units
Ⓑ 30 square units
Ⓒ 36 square units
Ⓓ 18 square units

4. **Calculate the area of the following polygon.**

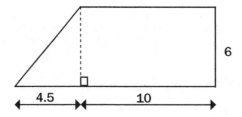

Ⓐ 60 square units
Ⓑ 73.5 square units
Ⓒ 13.5 square units
Ⓓ 24 square units

5. **What is the volume of the following triangular prism?**

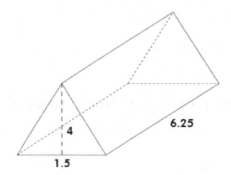

Ⓐ 11.75 cubic units
Ⓑ 20 cubic units
Ⓒ 37.5 cubic units
Ⓓ 18.75 cubic units

6. **What is the volume of a prism with the following base and a height of 2.75?**

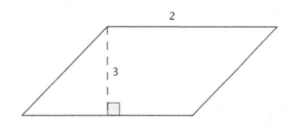

Ⓐ 8.25 cubic units
Ⓑ 13.75 cubic units
Ⓒ 16.5 cubic units
Ⓓ 8.75 cubic units

7. **What is the surface area of a cube with sides of length 2?**

    Ⓐ 16 square units
    Ⓑ 8 square units
    Ⓒ 24 square units
    Ⓓ 18 square units

8. **What is the surface area of a rectangular prism with dimensions 2, $\frac{1}{2}$, and $\frac{1}{4}$?**

    Ⓐ 2

    Ⓑ $\frac{13}{4}$

    Ⓒ $\frac{9}{4}$

    Ⓓ $\frac{3}{2}$

9. **Find the area of the shape below. (Round to the nearest tenth). Use pi = 3.14.**

    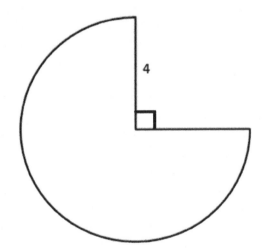

    Ⓐ 37.7 square units
    Ⓑ 50.2 square units
    Ⓒ 18.8 square units
    Ⓓ 35.2 square units

10. John has a container with a volume of 170 cubic feet filled with sand. He wants to transfer his sand into the new container shown below so he can store more sand. After he transfers the sand, how much more sand is remaining in the old container?

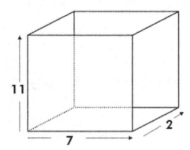

Ⓐ 16 cubic feet of sand
Ⓑ 26 cubic feet of sand
Ⓒ 150 cubic feet of sand
Ⓓ 324 cubic feet of sand

Chapter 4

Lesson 6: Angles

1. **Find x.**

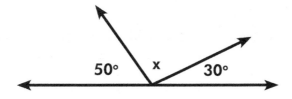

ⓐ 40°
ⓑ 60°
ⓒ 80°
ⓓ 100°

2. **Find the measures of the missing angles in the figure below.**

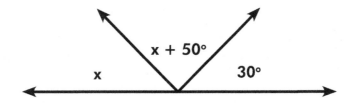

ⓐ 30° and 60°
ⓑ 60° and 90°
ⓒ 50° and 100°
ⓓ 60° and 120°

3. **The sum of the measures of angles a and b 155 degrees. What is the measure of angle b?**

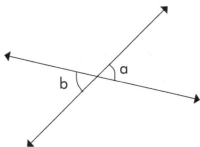

ⓐ 155 degrees
ⓑ 77.5 degrees
ⓒ 35 degrees
ⓓ 210.5 degrees

4. **What is true about every pair of vertical angles?**

    Ⓐ They are supplementary.
    Ⓑ They are complementary.
    Ⓒ They are equal in measure.
    Ⓓ They total 360 degrees.

5. **If the sum of the measures of two angles is 180 degrees, they are called ---**

    Ⓐ supplementary angles
    Ⓑ complementary angles
    Ⓒ vertical angles
    Ⓓ equivalent angles

6. **If angle a measures 30 degrees, what is the measure of angle b?**

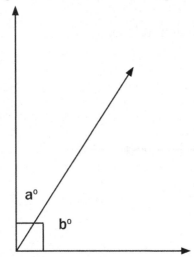

    Ⓐ 60 degrees
    Ⓑ 30 degrees
    Ⓒ 150 degrees
    Ⓓ 20 degrees

7. **If the measure of the first of two complementary angles is 68 degrees, what is the measure of the second angle?**

    Ⓐ 68 degrees
    Ⓑ 22 degrees
    Ⓒ 44 degrees
    Ⓓ 34 degrees

8. If the sum of the measures of angles a and b is 110 degrees, what is the measure of angle c?

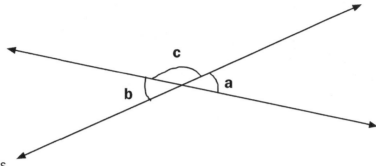

Ⓐ 125 degrees
Ⓑ 55 degrees
Ⓒ 70 degrees
Ⓓ 180 degrees

9. If two angles are both supplementary and equal in measure, they must be

Ⓐ vertical angles
Ⓑ right angles
Ⓒ adjacent angles
Ⓓ obtuse angles

10. If the sum of the measures of angles a and b is 240 degrees, what is the measure of angle c?

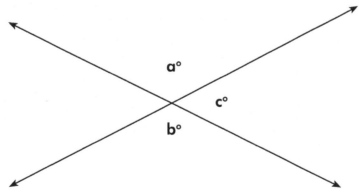

Ⓐ 60 degrees
Ⓑ 30 degrees
Ⓒ 160 degrees
Ⓓ 150 degrees

End of Geometry and Measurment

Answer Key and Detailed Explanations

Chapter 4: Geometry and Measurement

Lesson 1: Application of proportion and unit rates using measurement

Question No.	Answer	Detailed Explanations
1	B	There are 12 inches in a foot. $69 \text{ inches} * (\frac{1 \text{ foot}}{12 \text{ inches}}) = \frac{69}{12} = 5.75 \text{ feet}$
2	D	There are 4 quarts to a gallon. $7*4 = 28$ quarts $28 + 3 = 31$ quarts
3	D	There are 100 cm in a meter and 1000 meters in a kilometer. $3.7 \text{ km} * (\frac{1000 \text{ m}}{1 \text{ km}}) * (\frac{100 \text{ cm}}{1 \text{ m}}) = 370,000 \text{ cm}$
4	B	There are 16 ounces per pound. $136 \text{ ounces} * (\frac{1 \text{ lb}}{16 \text{ oz}}) = 8.5 \text{ pounds}$
5	C	There are 8 ounces per cup, 2 cups per pint, 2 pints per quart and 4 quarts per gallon. $5 \text{ gal} * (\frac{4 \text{ qts}}{1 \text{ gal}}) * (\frac{2 \text{ pints}}{1 \text{ qt}}) * (\frac{2 \text{ cups}}{1 \text{ pt}}) * (\frac{8 \text{ oz}}{1 \text{ cup}}) = 640 \text{ ounces}$
6	B	Find the total length of the race in meters: $1284 + 1635 + 1473 = 4392$ meters There are 1000 meters in 1 kilometer. $4392 \text{ m} * (\frac{1 \text{ km}}{1000 \text{ m}}) = 4.392 = 4.4 \text{ km}$
7	C	Find the total number of minutes for the month: 1 h 3 m + 1 h 18 m + 55 m + 68 m = 63 m + 78 m + 55 m + 68 m = 264 minutes. There are 60 minutes in 1 hour. $264 \text{ min} * (\frac{1 \text{ hr}}{60 \text{ min}}) = 4.4 \text{ hours}$
8	C	There are 60 minutes in 1 hour. 3 miles/18 minutes = x miles/60 minutes $3*60 = 18*x$ $180 = 18x$ Divide both side by 18 x = 10 miles per hour
9	B	Find the perimeter by adding all four sides of the garden: $67 + 67 + 92 + 92 = 318$ in There are 12 inches in a foot. $318 \text{ in} * (\frac{1 \text{ foot}}{12 \text{ in}}) = 26.5 \text{ feet}$

Question No.	Answer	Detailed Explanations
10	B	There are 100 cm in a meter and 2.54 cm in 1 inch. 1.27 meters * $(\frac{100\ cm}{1\ m})$ * $(\frac{1\ in}{2.54\ cm})$ = 50 inches 50 in / 12 in = 4.17 feet = 4 feet 2 inches

Lesson 2: Drawing Plane (2-D) Figures

Question No.	Answer	Detailed Explanations
1	D	The sum of any two sides of a triangle is always greater than the third side. Here, the sum of $1 + 1 = 2$. Since the sum of $1 + 1$ is not greater than 2, the lengths given cannot be the side lengths of a triangle.
2	C	The sum of any two sides of a triangle is always greater than the third side. Here, the sum of $4 + 8.5 = 12.5$. Since the sum of $4 + 8.5$ is not greater than 14, the lengths given cannot be the side lengths of a triangle.
3	A	The sum of the measure of angles in a triangle is always 180°. To find a missing angle, add the known angles and subtract the sum from 180°. (1) $100 + 60 = 160$ (2) $180 - 160 = 20$. Therefore, the measure of the third angle is 20°.
4	D	Triangles classified by angles are acute (all acute angles), obtuse (one obtuse angle), or right (one right angle). Triangles classified by sides are scalene (no equal sides), isosceles (two equal sides) or equilateral (three equal sides).
5	A	The answer is a. In triangles, the smallest angle (by degree measure) is always across from the shortest side. Since 8 is the length of the shortest side, a is the smallest angle because it is across from 8.
6	B	The sum of the measures of the angles in a triangle is always 180°. To find a missing angle, add the known angles and solve for x. (1) $70 + 13x + 9x = 180$ (2) $70 + 22x = 180$ (now subtract 70 from both sides) (3) $22x = 110$ (divide each side by 22) (4) $x = 5$
7	D	The sum of any two sides of a triangle is always greater than the third side. Here, the sum of $2 + 2 = 4$. Since the sum of $2 + 2$ is not greater than 4, the lengths given cannot be the side lengths of a triangle.
8	A	Since the triange is an isosceles triangle, the unknown angles are equal. Let each unkown angle be x. ; $x + x + 70 = 180$ (Sum of angles of a triangle add upto 180). ; $2x + 70 = 180$. ; $2x = 110$ (Subtract 70 from both sides). ; $x = \dfrac{110}{2}$ (Divide both sides by 2); $x = 55$. The answer is 55°.
9	A	When two lines intersect to form perpendicular lines, four 90° angles are created. Since 90° angles are also called right angles, a triangle that has one angle formed by perpendicular lines is a right triangle.
10	B	Triangles classified by angles are acute (all acute angles, which are angles less than 90°), obtuse (one obtuse angle), or right (one right angle). Triangles classified by sides are scalene (no equal sides), isosceles (two equal sides), or equilateral (three equal sides).

Lesson 3: Cirumference of a circle

Question No.	Answer	Detailed Explanations
1	C	The correct answer is 90°. Selecting 25° results from incorrectly applying the qualities of a circle graph to the circle (a whole circle represents 100%, so four equal parts equal 25% each). Choosing 180° is a result of measuring the angle of the line formed by dividing the circle into two equal parts (a straight line measures 180°). A circle measures 360°, so the measure of each angle formed at the center would be less than 360°. By dividing it into 4 equal pieces, each angle will be 360 ÷ 4 = 90°.
2	C	The correct answer is 50.2 cm². To find the area of a circle, apply the formula $A = \pi r^2$. Since the problem gives the diameter of the circle, the first step is to find the radius by dividing the diameter by 2. 8 ÷ 2 = 4 cm. Next, plug in the numbers into the formula: (1) $\pi 4^2$ = (2) 3.14×4^2 = (3) 3.14×16 = (4) 50.24 cm² (5) 50.2 cm² (rounded to the nearest tenth). Common errors made when applying the area formula to circles are multiplying the radius by 2 instead of by itself (which would result in 25.1 cm²) or using the diameter of the circle to find the area (resulting in 201.0 cm²).
3	C	The correct answer is 20 cm. To find the radius when given the circumference of the circle, use $\frac{C}{2\pi}$, where C equals circumference. Insert the numbers from the problem, and solve: (1) $r = \frac{C}{2\pi}$ (2) 125 ÷ (2 x 3.14) = (3) 125 ÷ 6.28 = (4) 19.90 cm = (5) 20 cm (rounded to the nearest whole number). Finding a radius of 19 cm results from rounding down instead of rounding up. An answer of 10 cm results from dividing the radius by 2. Choosing 24 cm is based on adding 2 + π and dividing 125 by the sum.
4	A	The answer is 3.1 ft. Finding 3.2 ft results from rounding up instead of rounding down. A result of 0.8 ft comes from applying the formula for the area of a circle. Selecting 0.7 ft also results from using the area formula but also includes a rounding error. To apply the formula for the circumference of a circle, 2πr, plug in the given values, and solve. (1) 2πr (2) 2 × 3.14 × 0.5 (3) 6.28 × 0.5 = (4) 3.14 ft = (5) 3.1 ft (rounded to the nearest tenth).
5	B	The answer is 1 square unit. Area is defined as the number of square units that cover a specific space. Since the question calls for the area of a circle, the best answer is 1 square unit.

Question No.	Answer	Detailed Explanations
6	A	The answer is 26.2 square centimeters. First, find the area of the entire circle by applying the area formula —> $A = \pi r^2$. (1) $A = 3.14 \times 10^2 = 3.14 \times 100 = 314$ cm². Next, calculate the number of square centimeters per degree by dividing the area of the circle by the number of degrees in the circle. (2) $314 \div 360 = 0.87$ cm² per degree. Multiply the quotient by 30 and round to the nearest tenth. (3) $30 \times 0.87 = 26.16$ square centimeters (4) 26.2 cm² (rounded to the nearest tenth).
7	B	The correct answer is 24.6 cm². Area of a circle is given by $A = \pi r^2$, plug in the given values, and solve. $A = 3.14 \times 2.8^2 = 3.14 \times 7.84 = 24.61$ cm². Thus, area of the circle is 24.6 cm² (rounded to the nearest tenth).
8	A	The answer is 4 cm. To apply the formula for finding radius when given area of a circle, which is the square root of A/π, plug in the given values and solve. $r =$ square root of $A/\pi =$ square root of $(50 \div 3.14) =$ square root $(15.92) = 3.99$ cm. Thus, $r = 4$ cm (rounded to the nearest whole number).
9	D	The answer is 25.1 in. To apply the formula for circumference of a circle, $2\pi r$, plug in the given values and solve. Then, divide the circumference by 2 to find the circumference of the semi-circle. Circumference of Circle = $2\pi r$ $C = 2 \times 3.14 \times 8$ $= 6.28 \times 8 = 50.24$ Circumference of semicircle = $50.24 \div 2$ $= 25.12$ in $= 25.1$ in (rounded to the nearest tenth) Alternate Method : Perimeter of a semi-circle = $\pi r = 3.14 \times 8 = 25.12$ = 25.1 in (rounded to the nearest tenth).
10	C	An answer of 4 m results from calculating the radius by dividing $50.24 \div 3.14$ and then finding the square root of the quotient, 16. Selecting 6 m results from following the preceding steps, but then adding 4 + 2. Choosing 16 m is the result of dividing $50.24 \div 3.14$. In order to find the diameter, apply the formula for diameter after finding the radius. The formula is $d = 2r$ (diameter = 2 × radius). As mentioned, the radius is 4 m. Therefore, $4 \times 2 = 8$ m.

Lesson 4: Solve mathematical and real-world problems

Question No.	Answer	Detailed Explanations
1	D	Remember: In order to solve a similarity question, set up a proportion with corresponding sides, and solve!: $\frac{x}{12} = \frac{35}{15}$ or $\frac{x}{12} = \frac{21}{9}$. You can use cross products (ad = bc) to solve for x. (1) $\frac{x}{12} = \frac{35}{15}$ (2) 15x = (35)(12) (3) 15x = 420 (4) x = 420 ÷ 15 (5) x = 28
2	A	If the similarity ratio is $\frac{3}{2}$, then the ratio of the areas is the square of that ratio: $\frac{3}{2} \times \frac{3}{2} = \frac{9}{4}$.
3	A	In order to solve a similarity problem, set up a proportion with corresponding sides: $\frac{8}{4} = \frac{16}{8}$. Both ratios in simplest form are $\frac{2}{1}$. Therefore, the similarity ratio is $\frac{2}{1}$.
4	A	You can use cross products (ad = bc) to solve for x. (inch)/(miles) = (inch)/(miles) (1) $\frac{1}{5} = \frac{3}{x}$ (2) 1x = (3)(5) (3) x = 15 Therefore, the towns are 15 miles apart.
5	C	Corresponding angles are congruent in similar figures. Thus, the angles will have the same measures in the second figure as in the first.
6	A	A square pyramid consists of a square base and 4 triangular sides (for a total of 5 faces); therefore, the cross section of a pyramid would show a square.
7	A	A prism consists of two congruent bases and various congruent faces; therefore, the cross sections of a prism must show congruent polygons.
8	A	In order to form a cube, the nets must fold together to make the shape. Here, the figure would not form a cube when folded together to make a three-dimensional figure.
9	B	Horizontal cross section of a pentagonal prism is a pentagon.
10	A	A cube is a rectangular prism with four lateral faces and two bases (also faces) which are square. Therefore, the cross section of a cube is a square.

Lesson 5: Finding Area, Volume, & Surface Area

Question No.	Answer	Detailed Explanations
1	C	The answer is 27.09 square centimeters. To calculate the area of a rectangle, multiply the length and width. Multiplying $6.3 \times 4.3 = 27.09$ square centimeters.
2	D	The answer is 512 in³. The formula for the volume for a cube is $V = s^3$, where s is the length of one side. Multiplying $8 \times 8 \times 8 = 512$ in³.
3	A	The correct answer is 15 square units. To find the correct answer, apply the formula for the area of a triangle, $A = \frac{1}{2}bh$. First, calculate the base by adding $6 + 4 = 10$. Next, multiply the base times the height: $10 \times 3 = 30$. Then, divide the product by 2: $30 \div 2 = 15$ square units.
4	B	The answer is 73.5 square units. This is a compound figure comprised of a triangle and a rectangle. Identify the length and width of rectangle. Apply the formula for area of a rectangle, $A = bh$ or $A = lw$, and the formula for the area of a triangle, $A = \frac{1}{2}bh$. Then, add the two products together. The sum is the total area of the figure. (1) area of rectangle: $6 \times 10 = 60$ square units (2) area of triangle : $(\frac{1}{2}) \times 4.5 \times 6 = 13.5$ square units (3) $60 + 13.5 = 73.5$ square units
5	D	The answer is 18.75 cubic units. The formula for volume is $V = BH$, where B = the area of the base, and H = height. Since the base is a triangle, the formula is $V = (\frac{1}{2}bh)(H)$. To solve, plug in the numbers: $V = (\frac{1}{2}bh)(H) = (\frac{1}{2} \times 1.5 \times 4)(6.25) = (3)(6.25) = 18.75$ cubic units.
6	C	The answer is 16.5 cubic units. The formula for volume is $V = BH$, where B = the area of the base, and H = height. Since the base is a parallelogram, the formula is $V = (bh)(H)$. To solve, plug in the numbers: $V = (bh)(H) = (2 \times 3)(2.75) = (6)(2.75) = 16.5$ cubic units.
7	C	A cube has 6 square faces. In this particular cube, each face has an area of $2 \times 2 = 4$ square units. The overall surface area $= 6 \times 4 = 24$ square units
8	B	This prism is made up of 6 rectangles. Two of them are 2 by 0.5, two of them are 2 by 0.25, and two of them are 0.5 by 0.25 The surface area $= 2(2)(0.5) + 2(2)(0.25) + 2(0.5)(0.25) = 3.25$ square units, or $\frac{13}{4}$ square units.

Question No.	Answer	Detailed Explanations
9	A	The answer is 37.7 square units. First, find the area of the entire circle by applying the area formula—πr^2. Next, multiply the area by $\frac{3}{4}$ in order to find the area of the shape. (1) πr^2 (2) $3.14 \times 4^2 =$ (3) $3.14 \times 16 =$ (4) Area $= 50.24$ cm² (5) $50.24 \times \frac{3}{4} = 37.68 =$ (6) $37.68 = 37.7$ cm²
10	A	Volume of the new container $= l \times w \times h = 7 \times 2 \times 11 = 154$ cubic feet. Therefore, after transferring the sand, amount of sand remaining in the old container $= 170 - 154 = 16$ cubic feet.

Lesson 6: Angles

Question No.	Answer	Detailed Explanations
1	D	The answer is 100°. Reminder: Angles that together form a straight line are called supplementary, meaning they add to 180 degrees. In this case, 50 + x + 30 = 180 requires an x value of 100 degrees.
2	C	The answer is 50° and 100°. Angles that together form a straight line are supplementary, meaning their measures add to 180 degrees. In this case, x + (x + 50) + 30 = 180 can only be satisfied by an x value of 50, resulting in angles of measure 50 and 100 degrees.
3	B	The answer is 77.5 degrees. When two lines intersect, they form vertical angles, which are equal in measure. Angle a and angle b are vertical angles. To find the value of angle b, divide 155 by 2. The quotient is the value of angle b: 155 ÷ 2 = 77.5 degrees.
4	C	Vertical angles are congruent angles formed by two intersecting lines. The sum of the angles can be less than or greater than 90 degrees and 180 degrees, respectively, so they are not necessarily complementary or supplementary angles. Also, vertical angles do not form a complete circle, so they do not total 360 degrees.
5	A	Two angles are supplementary if the sum of their measures is equal to 180°. The sum of the measures of the angles cannot be greater than or less than 180°. It must be exactly 180°.
6	A	The answer is 60°. Angles a and b form a right angle, which measures 90°. This means that angles a and b are complementary. To find the measure of angle b, subtract the measure of angle a from 90: 90 - 30 = 60. Therefore, the measure of angle b is 60°.
7	B	The answer is 22°. Two angles are complementary if the sum of the measures of the angles equals 90°. To find the measure of the second angle, subtract the measure of the first angle from 90: 90 - 68 = 22. Therefore, the measure of the second angle is 22°.
8	A	The answer is 125 degrees. When two lines intersect to form vertical angles, the opposite angles are equal in measure. Angle a and angle b are vertical angles. To find the value of angle a, divide 110 by 2. The quotient is the value of angle a: 110 ÷ 2 = 55 degrees. Two intersecting lines also form adjacent supplementary angles which add up to 180°. Since angle a and angle c are adjacent and supplementary, subtract 55 from 180 to find the measure of angle c: 180 - 55 = 125.

Question No.	Answer	Detailed Explanations
9	B	Two angles are supplementary if the sum of the measures of the angles equals 180°. Since right angles are 90°, the sum of two right angles is 180°. Therefore, two right angles form supplementary angles.
10	A	The answer is 60 degrees. When two lines intersect to form vertical angles, the opposite angles are equal in measure. Angle a and angle b are vertical angles. To find the value of angle a and angle b, divide 240 by 2: 240 ÷ 2 = 120 degrees. Two intersecting lines also form adjacent supplementary angles, which add up to 180 degrees. Since angle a and angle c are adjacent and supplementary, subtract 120 from 180 to find the measure of angle c: 180 - 120 = 60.

Chapter 5

Data Analysis

Chapter 5

Lesson 1: Graphs

1.

Class Survey Should there be a field trip?		
	Yes	**No**
Mr. A's class	ⅼⅼⅼⅼ ⅼⅼⅼⅼ ⅼⅼⅼⅼ	ⅼⅼⅼⅼ ⅼⅼ
Mr. B's class	ⅼⅼⅼⅼ ⅼⅼⅼⅼ ⅼⅼⅼⅼ	ⅼⅼⅼⅼ ⅼⅼⅼⅼ ⅼⅼⅼ
Mr. C's class	ⅼⅼⅼⅼ ⅼⅼⅼⅼ ⅼ	ⅼⅼⅼⅼ ⅼⅼⅼⅼ ⅼ
Mr. D's class	ⅼⅼⅼⅼ ⅼⅼⅼⅼ ⅼⅼ	ⅼⅼⅼⅼ ⅼⅼⅼⅼ

Four 3rd grade classes in Hill Elementary School were surveyed to find out if they wanted to go on a field trip at the end of the school year. The tally table above was used to record the votes.
How many kids voted "Yes" in Mrs. B's class?

Ⓐ 28 kids
Ⓑ 15 kids
Ⓒ 13 kids
Ⓓ 23 kids

2.

Should there be a field trip?		
	Yes	**No**
Mr. A's class	14	7
Mr. B's class	15	13
Mr. C's class	11	11
Mr. D's class	12	10
Total	52	41

Four 3rd grade classes in Hill Elementary School were surveyed to find out if they wanted to go on a field trip at the end of the school year. The table above shows the results of the survey.
How many kids voted "Yes" in Mr. A's class?

Ⓐ 7 kids
Ⓑ 15 kids
Ⓒ 14 kids
Ⓓ 21 kids

3.

Should there be a field trip?		
	Yes	**No**
Mr. A's class	14	7
Mr. B's class	15	13
Mr. C's class	11	11
Mr. D's class	12	10
Total	52	41

Four 3rd grade classes in Hill Elementary School were surveyed to find out if they wanted to go on a field trip at the end of the school year. The table above shows the results of the survey.
How many kids altogether voted "No" for the field trip?

Ⓐ 82 kids
Ⓑ 11 kids
Ⓒ 52 kids
Ⓓ 41 kids

4. The students in Mr. Donovan's class were surveyed to find out their favorite school subjects. The results are shown in the pictograph. Use the pictograph to answer the following question:
How many students chose either science or math?

Our Favorite Subjects

Math	○○○○
Reading	○○
Science	○○○
History	○
Other	○○

Key: ○ = 2 votes

Ⓐ 6 students
Ⓑ 7 students
Ⓒ 14 students
Ⓓ 2 students

5.

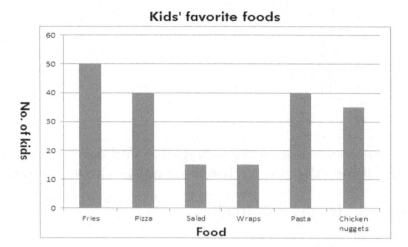

The third graders in Valley Elementary School were asked to pick their favorite food from 6 choices. The results are shown in the bar graph.
Which food was the favorite of the most children?

Ⓐ Pizza
Ⓑ Pasta
Ⓒ Fries
Ⓓ Salad

6. The sixth graders at Kilmer Middle School can choose to participate in one of the four music activities offered. The number of students participating in each activity is shown in the bar graph below. Use the information shown to answer the question.

There are 132 students who participate in music activities. What percentage of students who participate in music activities participate in chorus or jass band?

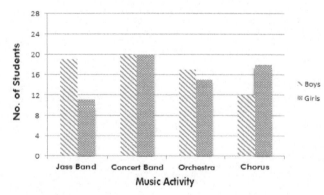

Ⓐ 45%
Ⓑ 38%
Ⓒ 40%
Ⓓ 50%

7. A.J. has downloaded 400 songs onto his computer. The songs are from a variety of genres. The circle graph below shows the breakdown of his collection by genre. Use the information shown to answer the question.

Which two genres together make up more than half of A.J.'s collection?

A.J.'s Music Collections

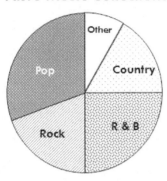

Ⓐ R + B and Country
Ⓑ Country and Rock
Ⓒ Rock and Pop
Ⓓ Pop and R + B

8. The results of the class' most recent science test are displayed in this histogram. Use the results to answer the question.

What percentage of the class scored an 81-90 on the test?

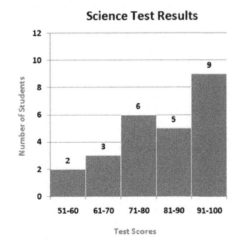

Ⓐ 5%
Ⓑ 20%
Ⓒ 25%
Ⓓ 30%

9. **How much of the graph do undergarments and socks make up together?**

Clothing Sales Breakdown

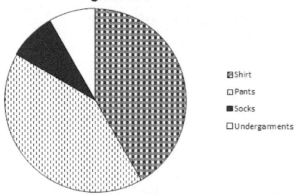

- Shirt
- Pants
- Socks
- Undergarments

Ⓐ less than 5%
Ⓑ between 5% and 10%
Ⓒ between 10% and 25%
Ⓓ more than 25%

10. **As part of their weather unit, the students in Mr. Green's class prepared a line graph showing the high and low temperatures recorded each day during a one-week period. Use the graph to answer the question.**

What percentage of the days had a temperature 80 degrees or higher? Round to the nearest tenth.

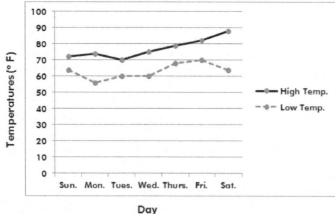

Ⓐ 14.3%
Ⓑ 42.9%
Ⓒ 28.6%
Ⓓ None of these

Chapter 5

Lesson 2: Mean, Median, and Mean Absolute Deviation

1. **Consider the following dot-plot for Height versus Weight.**

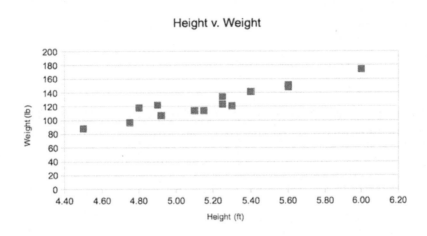

Height v. Weight

What does this dot-plot indicate about the correlation between height and weight?

Ⓐ There is no correlation.
Ⓑ There is a strong negative correlation.
Ⓒ There is a strong positive correlation.
Ⓓ There is a weak positive correlation.

2. **The following chart represents the heights of boys on the basketball and soccer teams.**

Basketball	Soccer
5'4''	4'11''
5'2''	4'10''
5'3''	5'9''
5'5''	5'1''
5'5''	5'0''
5'1''	5'1''
5'9''	5'3''
5'3''	5'1''

What inference can be made based on this information?

Ⓐ Soccer players have a higher average skill level than basketball players.
Ⓑ Soccer players have a lower average weight than basketball players.
Ⓒ Basketball players have a higher average height than soccer players.
Ⓓ No inference can be made.

3. Use the table below to answer the question that follows:

Month	Avg Temp.
January	24°F
February	36°F
March	55°F
April	65°F
May	72°F
June	78°F

What is the difference between the mean temperature of the first four months of the year and the mean temperature of the next two months?

Ⓐ 15 degrees
Ⓑ 20 degrees
Ⓒ 25 degrees
Ⓓ 30 degrees

4. Use the table below to answer the question:

Month	Avg Temp.
January	24°F
February	36°F
March	55°F
April	65°F
May	72°F
June	78°F

If the temperature in January was 54°F instead of 24°F, by how much would the mean temperature for the six months increase?

Ⓐ 5°F
Ⓑ 10°F
Ⓒ 30°F
Ⓓ 35°F

5. **Use the table to answer the question below:**

Team	Wins
Mustangs	14
Spartans	17
North Stars	16
Hornets	9
Stallions	13
Renegades	9
Rangers	5

What is the mode of the wins for all the teams in the above table?

(A) 14
(B) 5
(C) 13
(D) 9

6. **Jack scored 7, 9, 2, 6, 15 and 15 points in 6 basketball games. Find the mean, median and mode scores for all the games.**

(A) Mean = 7, Median = 9 and Mode = 2
(B) Mean = 9, Median = 7 and Mode = 15
(C) Mean = 9, Median = 8 and Mode = 15
(D) Mean = 7, Median = 2 and Mode = 9

7. **Mean absolute deviation is a measure of...**

(A) Central Tendency
(B) Variability
(C) Averages
(D) Sample Size

8. **Calculate the mean for the following set of data:**

$$\left\{\frac{7}{4}, \frac{3}{4}, \frac{5}{4}, \frac{7}{4}, \frac{3}{4}, \frac{5}{4}\right\}$$

Ⓐ $\dfrac{7}{4}$

Ⓑ $\dfrac{5}{2}$

Ⓒ $\dfrac{5}{4}$

Ⓓ $\dfrac{1}{6}$

9. **Another word for mean is...**

Ⓐ Average
Ⓑ Middle
Ⓒ Most
Ⓓ Count

10. **What is the median for the following set of data?**

$$\left\{\frac{4}{5}, \frac{1}{3}, \frac{1}{3}, \frac{1}{5}, \frac{2}{3}\right\}$$

Ⓐ $\dfrac{1}{3}$

Ⓑ $\dfrac{2}{3}$

Ⓒ $\dfrac{1}{5}$

Ⓓ $\dfrac{1}{4}$

Chapter 5

Lesson 3: Sampling a Population

1. **Joe and Mary want to calculate the average height of students in their school. Which of the following groups of students would produce the least amount of bias?**

    Ⓐ Every student in the 8th grade.
    Ⓑ Every student on the school basketball team.
    Ⓒ A randomly selected group of students in the halls.
    Ⓓ Joe & Mary's friends.

2. **Which of the following represents who you should survey in a population?**

    Ⓐ A random, representative group from the population
    Ⓑ Every individual in a population
    Ⓒ Only those in the population that agree with you
    Ⓓ Anyone, including those not in the population

3. **What does increasing the sample size of a survey do for the overall results?**

    Ⓐ Decreases bias in the results
    Ⓑ Increases the mean of the results
    Ⓒ Increases the reliability of the results
    Ⓓ Increasing sample size does not impact the results of a survey

4. **Which of the following is not a valid reason for not surveying everyone in a population?**

    Ⓐ It takes a far longer amount of time to survey everyone.
    Ⓑ Not everyone will be willing to participate in the survey.
    Ⓒ It is hard to determine the exact size of a population necessary to ensure everyone is surveyed.
    Ⓓ Surveying everyone produces unreliable results.

5. **Why is it important to know the sample size of a given survey?**

    Ⓐ It helps determine whether any bias exists.
    Ⓑ It helps determine how reliable the results are.
    Ⓒ It gives a good estimate for the size of the target population.
    Ⓓ It is not important to know the sample size.

6. **John and Maggie want to calculate the average height of students in their school. Which of the following groups of students would most likely produce the most amount of bias?**

Ⓐ Every student in the 8th grade.
Ⓑ Every student on the school basketball team.
Ⓒ A randomly selected group of students in the halls.
Ⓓ John & Maggie's friends.

7. **Which of the following question types will provide the most useful statistical results?**

Ⓐ Open-ended questions where the person surveyed can answer in any way they want
Ⓑ Multiple choice questions offering the person a representative number of choices
Ⓒ True or false questions

8. **Which of the following does not represent a way of avoiding bias in survey results?**

Ⓐ Use neutral words in the questions asked
Ⓑ Ensure a random sample of the population
Ⓒ Only survey individuals that will answer a certain way
Ⓓ Tailor the conclusions based on survey results, not previous thoughts

9. **The following data set represents survey results on a scale of 1 to 10.**

   {8, 8, 9, 8, 6, 7, 7, 7, 8, 8, 6}

   Which of the following survey result would you be most surprised with if given by the next person surveyed?

   Ⓐ 6
   Ⓑ 5
   Ⓒ 8
   Ⓓ 7

10. **The following data set represents survey results on a scale of 1 to 10.**

   {6, 6, 7, 6, 8, 7, 7, 7, 6, 6, 8}

   Which of the following survey results would you be most surprised with if given by the next person surveyed?

   Ⓐ 6
   Ⓑ 10
   Ⓒ 8
   Ⓓ 7

Chapter 5

Lesson 4: Compare two populations based on data in random samples

1. The following data set represents a score from 1-10 for a customers' experience at a local restaurant.

    { 1, 1, 2, 1, 3, 4, 7, 8, 1, 3, 4, 2, 1, 3, 7, 2 }

    If a score of 1 means the customer did not have a good experience, and a 10 means the customer had a fantastic experience, what can you infer by looking at the data?

    Ⓐ Overall, customers had a good experience.
    Ⓑ Overall, customers had a bad experience.
    Ⓒ Overall, customers had an "ok" experience.
    Ⓓ Nothing can be inferred from this data.

2. The manager of a local pizza place has asked you to make suggestions on how to improve his menu. The following bar graph represents the results of a survey asking customers what their favorite food at the restaurant was.

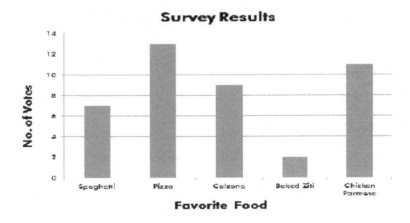

    Based on these survey results, which menu item would you suggest the manager remove from the menu?

    Ⓐ Spaghetti
    Ⓑ Pizza
    Ⓒ Calzone
    Ⓓ Baked Ziti

3. **What are the measures of central tendency?**

   Ⓐ Mean, Median, Mode
   Ⓑ Median, Mode, Mean Absolute Deviation
   Ⓒ Median, Mean Absolute Deviation, Sample Size
   Ⓓ Mean, Median, Range

4. **What is the mean absolute deviation for the following set of data?**

   {1, 2, 3, 4}

   Ⓐ 1
   Ⓑ 2.5
   Ⓒ 4
   Ⓓ 2

5. **What are the central tendencies of the following data set? (round to the nearest tenth)**

   {2, 2, 3, 4, 6, 8, 9, 10, 13, 13, 16, 17}

   Ⓐ Mean: 8.6, Median: 8.5, Mode: 2, 13
   Ⓑ Mean: 8.5, Median: 8.4, Mode: 2, 3
   Ⓒ Mean: 8.5, Median: 8.6, Mode: 2, 13
   Ⓓ Mean: 7.6, Median: 7.5, Mode: 10, 13

6. **John comes up with the following methods for generating unbiased samples from shoppers at a mall.**

   I. Ask random strangers in the mall

   II. Always go to the mall at the same time of day

   III. Go to different places in the mall

   IV. Don't ask questions the same way to different people

   Which of these techniques represents the best way of generating an unbiased sample?

   Ⓐ I and II
   Ⓑ I and III
   Ⓒ I, II, and III
   Ⓓ All of these

7. **These two samples are about students' favorite subjects. What inference can you make concerning the students' favorite subjects?**

Student samples	Science	Math	English Language Arts	Total
#1	40	14	30	84
#2	43	17	33	93

Ⓐ Students prefer Science over the other subjects.
Ⓑ Students prefer Math over the other subjects.
Ⓒ Students prefer English language arts over the other subjects.
Ⓓ Students prefer History over the other subjects.

8. **These two samples are about students' favorite types of movies. What inference can you make concerning the students' favorite types of movies?**

Student samples	Comedy	Action	Drama	Total
#1	35	45	19	99
#2	38	48	22	108

Ⓐ Students prefer action movies over the other types.
Ⓑ Students prefer drama over the other types.
Ⓒ Students prefer comedy over the other types.
Ⓓ none

9. **These two samples are about students' favorite fruits. What inference can you make concerning the students' favorite fruits?**

Student samples	Blueberries	Bananas	Strawberries	Total
#1	33	18	44	95
#2	30	20	40	90

Ⓐ Students prefer strawberries over the other fruits.
Ⓑ Students prefer bananas over the other fruits.
Ⓒ Students prefer blueberries over the other fruits.
Ⓓ none

10. Jane and Matt conducted two surveys about students' favorite sports to play. What inference can you make concerning the students' favorite sports?

Student samples	Soccer	Basketball	Tennis	Total
#1	50	145	26	221
#2	56	150	20	226

Ⓐ Most students like basketball over soccer or tennis.
Ⓑ Most students like soccer over basketball or tennis.
Ⓒ Most students like tennis over soccer or basketball.
Ⓓ Most students like track.

End of Data Analysis

Answer Key and Detailed Explanations

Chapter 5: Data Analysis

Lesson 1: Graphs

Question No.	Answer	Detailed Explanations
1	B	The chart shows 3 sets of 5 tallies for Mrs. B's class in the "yes" column. Multiplying 3 x 5 the tallies represent 15 kids.
2	C	The number 14 in the "yes" column for Mrs. A's class represents 14 votes.
3	D	The "Total" row displays the overall number of votes. There is a total of 41 votes represented in the "No" column.
4	C	First, add the totals number of students who chose Science and Math. 3 + 4 = 7. The chart states that each object stands for 2 votes. Multiply the Science and Math total by 2. 7 x 2 = 14.
5	C	The tallest bar indicates the food that was chosen most often. That would be considered the "favorite."
6	A	Jazz Band: 19 +11 = 30 students Chorus: 12 + 18 = 30 students 60 students participate in either jazz band or chorus. To find the percentage, divide 60 by 132. $60 \div 132 \approx 0.45$ To change the decimal to a percent, move the decimal point to the right two places. $0.45 = 45\%$
7	D	Pop and R & B together would make up more than half of the pie chart, or above 50%.
8	B	5 students scored an 81-90 on the test out of 25 students. Convert this fraction into percentage. $\dfrac{5}{25} \times 100 = 20\%$
9	C	Socks and undergarments together appear to take up more than a tenth, but less than a quarter, of the pie chart. The percentage would be between 10% and 25%.
10	C	Friday and Saturday both had temperatures of 80 degrees or higher. That means that $\dfrac{2}{7}$ days were 80 degrees or more. Convert $\dfrac{2}{7}$ into percentage by multiplying $\dfrac{2}{7}$ with 100. $\dfrac{2}{7} \times 100 = 28.57\%$ Round to the nearest tenth making the percentage 28.6%

Lesson 2: Mean, Median, and Mean Absolute Deviation

Question No.	Answer	Detailed Explanations
1	C	There is a strong positive correlation between the height and the weight because there is an upward trend in the weight as a person gets taller.
2	C	When analyzing the heights of the basketball players and soccer players, the average height of the basketball players is 5'4, and the average height of the soccer players is 5'2. Therefore, the average height of the basketball players is higher than the average height of the soccer players.
3	D	Remember: the mean represents the average of the values, which is calculated by adding all the values together then dividing by the number of values you added. In this case, $\frac{24 + 36 + 55 + 65}{2} = 45$, and $\frac{72 + 78}{2} = 75$. The difference between these two values is 30, as indicated.
4	A	Remember: A mean is the average of all the data presented. In this case, you have to average the temperatures, then replace the January temperature with 54 and recalculate the average, then take the difference. Another way of solving the problem is as follows: January temperature has increased by 54 - 24 = 30 degrees. So, this 30 degrees is to be distributed equally among all the six months. Therefore the average temperature increases by $\frac{30}{6} = 5$ degrees.
5	D	Remember: the mode of a set of data is the number that occurs most frequently. For this set of data, that number is 9.
6	C	Remember: Mean is the average, median is the middle-number when data is arranged numerically, and mode is the number that appears most often.
7	B	Mean absolute deviation is a measure of the distance between each data value and the mean, so it measures variability.
8	C	To find the mean, add the values, and divide that value by the amount of numbers in the data set. (1) The sum is $\frac{30}{4}$ (2) $\frac{30}{4} \div \frac{6}{1} =$ (3) $\frac{30}{4} \times \frac{1}{6} = \frac{30}{24}$ (the GCF of 30 and 24 is 6) (4) $\frac{5}{4}$
9	A	Mean is the average of a set of data; therefore, another word for mean is average.

Question No.	Answer	Detailed Explanations
10	A	To find the median, find the middle number in the data set. One way to find the median is to order the numbers from least to greatest and cross out the numbers until the middle is reached. Here, the middle number is $\frac{1}{3}$. Calculation: To compare fractions, we have to rewrite them with common denominator. Here LCM of 3 and 5 is 15. Rewrite all the fractions with 15 as the denominator. $\frac{4}{5} = \frac{4 \times 3}{5 \times 3} = \frac{12}{15}$. $\frac{1}{3} = \frac{1 \times 5}{3 \times 5} = \frac{5}{15}$. $\frac{1}{5} = \frac{1 \times 3}{5 \times 3} = \frac{3}{15}$. $\frac{2}{3} = \frac{2 \times 5}{3 \times 5} = \frac{10}{15}$. $\frac{3}{15} < \frac{5}{15} < \frac{10}{15} < \frac{12}{15}$. Therefore, when we arrange the data in ascending order, we get $\frac{1}{5}, \frac{1}{3}, \frac{1}{3}, \frac{2}{3}, \frac{4}{5}$. Median is 3rd score, which is $\frac{1}{3}$.

Lesson 3: Sampling a Population

Question No.	Answer	Detailed Explanations
1	C	A group of randomly selected students in the hallways would produce the least amount of bias because it is unlikely for assumptions to be made or factors that influence the data to be present. For example, students in the 8th grade may be taller than other students in other grades, skewing the data toward a higher average. A similar assumption can be made about students on the basketball team. Joe and Mary would already have an idea of the height of their friends.
2	A	A random, representative group represents the people to survey in a population because each person in the population has an equal chance of being included and there is less of a chance of bias altering the results of the survey.
3	C	As the size of the sample (people surveyed) increases, the results become more accurate. Therefore, increasing the sample size increases the reliability of the results.
4	D	Surveying everyone would produce reliable results because there would specific data from each person; however, due to the length of time needed, among other reasons, surveying everyone may not be possible (depending on the reasons for the survey).
5	B	A sample size gets information from a small group from the population. Since the sample size is supposed to represent the population at large, it's important to know the parameters of the sample size in order to determine how reliable the results are for a given survey.
6	B	An assumption can be made that students on the basketball team are likely to be taller than other students at the school, which can influence the results (make it appear that the average height of the general school population is higher than it actually is). Therefore, calculating the average height of the basketball team would most likely produce the most amount of bias.
7	B	Multiple choice questions are useful for statistical results because they can represents different amounts of data that can be separated into categories and sub-categories based on the type of survey and the intended outcome.

Question No.	Answer	Detailed Explanations
8	C	Bias in collecting data can be caused by using questions where there are likely to be assumptions made or factors that influence the data. A survey that asks questions that cause individuals to answer in a certain way makes assumptions and influences the outcome of the data. Therefore, using that type of survey does not avoid bias.
9	B	When analyzing the data, out of the 10 responses, none of the responses have been less than 6. Therefore, a surprising response from the next person would be a 5 since it is outside the range.
10	B	When analyzing the data, out of the 10 responses, all are within the range of 6 to 8. Therefore, a surprising response from the next person would be a 10 since it is outside of the range.

Lesson 4: Compare two populations based on data in random samples

Question No.	Answer	Detailed Explanations
1	B	Out of 16 scores, 13 of 16 are 4 or below. Since the majority of the scores are low, a person can infer that, overall, customers had a bad experience.
2	D	To answer this question, look at the results of the different dishes. Spaghetti: 7 Pizza: 13 Calzone: 9 Baked Ziti: 2 Since only 2 people said that baked ziti was their favorite food, it is the menu item the manager should remove from the menu.
3	A	The measures of central tendency are mean, which is the average of a set of data; median, which is the middle of a set of data, and mode, which is the value which appears most in a set of data.
4	A	To find the mean absolute deviation, (1) find the mean, (2) find the difference between each data value and the mean (since we are interested in deviation only, ignore the negative sign in the difference before taking average), and (3) average the differences. Here, the mean is 2.5. The differences between the data value and the mean are 1.5, 0.5, 0.5, and 1.5. The average is 1.
5	A	Since mode is the value that appears most in a set of data, the original list has two modes of 2 and 13 because each value appears the same number of times. Find the mean by adding the set of values and dividing by the amount of numbers in the set of data: (1) $2 + 2 + 3 + 4 + 6 + 8 + 9 + 10 + 13 + 13 + 16 + 17 = 103$ (2) $\frac{103}{12} = 8.6$ To find the median, find the middle number in the data set. One way to find the median is to order the numbers from least to greatest and cross out the numbers until the middle is reached. Here, the middle numbers are 8 and 9. Add the numbers together, and divide by 2. (1) $8 + 9 = 17$ (2) $17 \div 2 = 8.5$
6	B	A group of randomly selected strangers in different places of a mall would produce the least amount of bias because there is unlikely to be assumptions made or factors that influence the data.
7	A	In the survey, 83 students selected science as their favorite subject while the other subjects had a combined number of 94 students. Therefore, an inference can be made that students prefer science over the other subjects.
8	A	In the sample, a combined 93 students chose action movies, 41 students chose drama, and 73 chose comedy. Therefore, an inference can be made that students prefer action movies to other types of movies.

Question No.	Answer	Detailed Explanations
9	A	In the sample, a combined 84 students chose strawberries, 38 students chose bananas and 63 chose blueberries. Therefore, an inference can be made that students prefer strawberries to other types of fruit.
10	A	In the sample, a combined 295 students chose basketball, 106 students chose soccer, and 46 students chose play tennis. Since more students chose basketball, an inference can be made that most students like basketball over soccer or tennis.

STAAR FAQs

What will STAAR Math Assessment Look Like?

In many ways, the STAAR assessments will be unlike anything many students have ever seen. The tests will be conducted online, requiring students complete tasks to assess a deeper understanding of the Texas Essential Knowledge and Skills (TEKS).

The STAAR assessments are designed so that students can complete the 3rd–5th grade assessments in two hours and the 6th–8th grade assessments in three hours. If needed, students can take up to four hours to complete their assessment. The testing time begins after all directions are read to the students. Students may be allowed to take breaks during testing, potentially including breaks for snacks or meals.

How is this Lumos tedBook aligned to STAAR Guidelines?

The practice tests provided in the Lumos Program were created to reflect the depth and rigor of the State of Texas Assessment of Academic Readiness based on the information published by the test administrator. However, the content and format of the State of Texas Assessment of Academic Readiness that is officially administered to the students could be different compared to these practice tests.

What Question types are included in the Online STAAR?

The question types that you will encounter on the Texas STAAR assessments are:

In Math:
Multiple Choice Single Answer
Grid in

In ELA:
Multiple Choice Single Answer
Constructed Response (only in Writing tests for Grade 4 and Grade 7)

For more information on 2021-22 Assessment year, visit
http://www.lumoslearning.com/a/STAAR-2021-faqs
OR Scan the **QR Code**

What is this STAAR Test Practice Book?

Inside this book, you will find practice sections aligned to each TEKS. Students will have the ability to review questions on each standard, one section at a time, in the order presented, or they can choose to study the sections where they need the most practice.

In addition to the practice sections, you will have access to two full-length practice tests online. Completing these tests will help students master the different areas that are included in newly aligned STAAR tests and practice test taking skills. The results will help the students and educators get insights into students' strengths and weaknesses in specific content areas. These insights could be used to help students strengthen their skills in difficult topics and to improve speed and accuracy while taking the test.

Because the STAAR assessment includes questions covering various TEKS standards, it is necessary for students to be able to regularly practice these questions. The Lumos online StepUp program provides practice tests that mimic the state assessments.

Discover Engaging and Relevant Learning Resources

Lumos EdSearch is a safe search engine specifically designed for teachers and students. Using EdSearch, you can easily find thousands of standards-aligned learning resources such as questions, videos, lessons, worksheets and apps. Teachers can use EdSearch to create custom resource kits to perfectly match their lesson objective and assign them to one or more students in their classroom.

To access the EdSearch tool, use the search box after you log into Lumos StepUp or use the link provided below.

http://www.lumoslearning.com/a/edsearchb	

The Lumos Standards Coherence map provides information about previous level, next level and related standards. It helps educators and students visually explore learning standards. It's an effective tool to help students progress through the learning objectives. Teachers can use this tool to develop their own pacing charts and lesson plans. Educators can also use the coherence map to get deep insights into why a student is struggling in a specific learning objective.

Teachers can access the Coherence maps after logging into the StepUp Teacher Portal or use the link provided below.

http://www.lumoslearning.com/a/coherence-map	

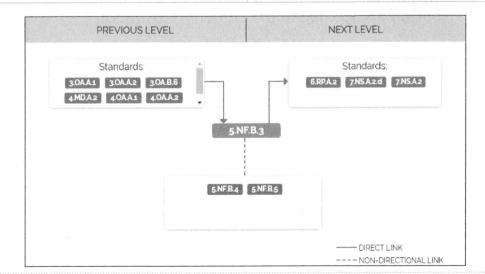

What if I buy more than one Lumos Study Program?

Step 1

Visit the URL and login to your account.
http://www.lumoslearning.com

Step 2

Click on 'My tedBooks' under the "Account" tab.
Place the Book Access Code and submit.

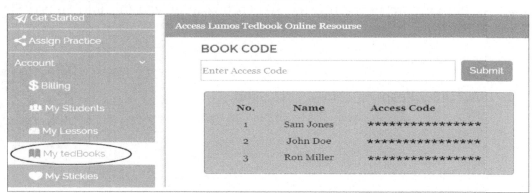

Step 3

To add the new book for a registered student, choose the
○ Existing Student button and select the student and submit.

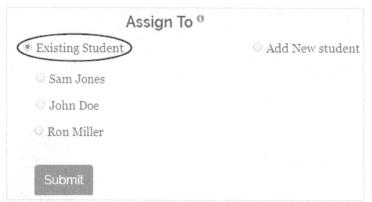

To add the new book for a new student, choose the ○ Add New student
button and complete the student registration.

Lumos StepUp® Mobile App FAQ For Students

What is the Lumos StepUp® App?

It is a FREE application you can download onto your Android Smartphones, tablets, iPhones, and iPads.

What are the Benefits of the StepUp® App?

This mobile application gives convenient access to Practice Tests, Common Core State Standards, Online Workbooks, and learning resources through your Smartphone and tablet computers.

- Eleven Technology enhanced question types in both MATH and ELA
- Sample questions for Arithmetic drills
- Standard specific sample questions
- Instant access to the Common Core State Standards
- Jokes and cartoons to make learning fun!

Do I Need the StepUp® App to Access Online Workbooks?

No, you can access Lumos StepUp® Online Workbooks through a personal computer. The StepUp® app simply enhances your learning experience and allows you to conveniently access StepUp® Online Workbooks and additional resources through your smartphone or tablet.

How can I Download the App?

Visit **lumoslearning.com/a/stepup-app** using your Smartphone or tablet and follow the instructions to download the app.

**QR Code
for Smartphone
Or Tablet Users**

Lumos StepUp® Mobile App FAQ For Parents and Teachers

What is the Lumos StepUp® App?

It is a free app that teachers can use to easily access real-time student activity information as well as assign learning resources to students. Parents can also use it to easily access school-related information such as homework assigned by teachers and PTA meetings. It can be downloaded onto smartphones and tablets from popular App Stores.

What are the Benefits of the Lumos StepUp® App?

It provides convenient access to

- Standards aligned learning resources for your students
- An easy to use Dashboard
- Student progress reports
- Active and inactive students in your classroom
- Professional development information
- Educational Blogs

How can I Download the App?

Visit **lumoslearning.com/a/stepup-app** using your Smartphone or tablet and follow the instructions to download the app.

QR Code
for Smartphone
Or Tablet Users

Progress Chart

Standard	Lesson	Page No.	Practice		Mastered	Re-practice /Reteach
TEKS			Date	Score		
7.6 (A)	Represent sample spaces for simple and compound events	11				
7.6 (B)	Simulate Compound Events to Estimate Probability	14				
7.6 (C)	Probability Models from Observed Frequencies	17				
7.6 (D)	Using Probability Models	20				
7.6 (H)	Problems using central tendency	23				
7.6 (I)	Determine experimental and theoretical probabilities	26				
7.3 (A)	Rational Numbers, Multiplication & Division	41				
7.3 (B)	Apply and extend previous understanding of operations to solve problems	43				
7.4 (A)	Represent proportions by equations	45				
7.4 (B)	Unit Rates	48				
7.4 (C)	Finding Constant of Proportionality	51				
7.4 (D)	Applying Ratios and Percents	54				
7.10 (A)	Modeling Using Equations or Inequalities	57				
7.10 (B)	Linear Inequality Word Problems	60				
7.10 (C)	Real world problem using inequality	63				
7.11 (B)	Equations and Inequalities	66				
7.4 (E)	Application of proportion and unit rates using measurement	86				
7.5 (A)	Drawing Plane (2-D) Figures	88				
7.5 (B)	Circumference of a circle	91				
7.5 (C)	Solve mathematical and real-world problems	93				
7.9 (A)	Finding Area, Volume, & Surface Area	97				
7.11 (C)	Angles	101				
7.6 (G)	Graphs	116				
7.12 (A)	Mean, Median, and Mean Absolute Deviation	121				
7.12 (B)	Sampling a Population	125				
7.12 (C)	Compare two populations based on data in random samples	127				

Grade 7

Lumos Learning
Developed by Expert Teachers

TEXAS
ENGLISH
LANGUAGE ARTS LITERACY
STAAR Practice

Updated for 2021-22

ONLINE

Two STAAR Practice Tests

COVERS 50+ SKILLS

Available
- At Leading book stores
- Online www.LumosLearning.com

Made in the USA
Coppell, TX
29 March 2022

75688557R00083